GENE SCHNAGL

MW01296073

FEAR KNOT

DEDICATION

This book is dedicated to my mother and father who taught me to enjoy and respect the outdoors, to respect our God, our nation, and each other.

To my wife and mate, Kathy, who gave me the opportunity to realize a dream and was willing to share it with me.

To Mickey, our black standard poodle, soul mate and friend, who had to leave us before we began our dream but was by our side and in our thoughts every nautical mile.

GENE SCHNAGL

Table of Contents

GENE SCHNAGL

FEAR KNOT

Have you ever sat in a quiet place and just done nothing but think? I would hope that at one time or another we all have. What is most important though is not that we are just sitting doing nothing, but the actual thoughts that are running through our head while we are doing it.

Living in Milwaukee, Wisconsin I have been blessed with a great "Thinking" spot. It's called the shores of beautiful Lake Michigan. Being a Great Lake's boater has allowed me an even better "Thinking" spot. I don't have to sit on the shore where the seagulls and geese decorate the grass. I can sit on the aft deck of my own boat and look out over the water. It is difficult to imagine anything as peaceful and relaxing as Lake Michigan on a quiet summer day. If you are a boater you know precisely what I mean about the serenity of the water. Water just has a natural soothing effect on us.

So, let's take a step back and I'll explain how our adventure over water all came about. One summer day in 2003, while I was sitting on the aft deck "Thinking" a boat pulled into the slip next to us. Yes, as I stated, I do a lot of thinking. According to my wife it's what I do best.

As I watched this boat pulling in I noticed a group of people standing on the dock to meet it and they all appeared to be pretty excited. They were all carrying balloons and "Welcome Home" signs. Now, being a professional "Thinker" I couldn't help but wonder what that was all about. It was later that I found out that the boat and its crew had just completed a yearlong trip on water called "America's Great Loop". Naturally my next thought was what the heck is that? I immediately struck up a conversation with the Captain of the vessel, Norm Naughton, and over time he was gracious enough to explain to me what this adventure was all about. Those conversations with Captain Naughton are what really got my wife and I started on a dream that opened a whole new world of boating to us.

So, just what is "America's Great Loop"? I guess the best way to describe it is a circumnavigation of the eastern United States via numerous, both natural and manmade, waterways. A number of these are The Great Lakes, navigable rivers, manmade canals, The Gulf of Mexico, the ICW and the Atlantic Ocean.

DEL CORONADO'S GREAT LOOP ROUTE

Having read that description you now understand exactly what The Loop is, right? If your answer is NO then you are just like me and you have to find out a lot more before considering undertaking a voyage like this. For me that need to know more information resulted in two years of preparation for the boat trip of a lifetime for my wife, Kathy, and I. I read everything I could find on the adventure in paperback and on the Internet. We joined the America's Great Loop Cruiser's Association which put us into direct contact with people from around the world with a similar dream. Those two years of preparation finally resulted in our living on our own boat for about ten months and traveling almost 7,000 miles over America's eastern waterways. A whole new life of boating had begun.

Just remember that not everyone is going to understand why you would want to undertake such a challenging adventure. To highlight this let me relate to you a statement made to me upon our return home.

I did have one boating friend state to me, "I just don't understand why everyone is getting so excited about what you guys did; after all, you just took a boat ride, right?" I guess I'll let you draw your own conclusions regarding whether we just took a boat ride or an adventure cruise. Did he really understand what we had just accomplished as a couple? Did he really understand what real boating was all about? Maybe some people just need to take a "boat ride" to be able to define what a "boat ride" is. We'll see!

Before beginning this writing I had to ask myself, why should I write a book, and if I do what should I write about? There are a lot of books out there to tell you how to prepare for and how to navigate a cruise like this. I just didn't think everyone needed one more book to take up space on their boat. I also knew I didn't want to write another, "what we did on our summer vacation" book.

It wasn't until the spring of 2012 that the answer regarding why to write a book came to me. At that time Kathy and I were attending the America's Great Loop Cruisers' Association Rendezvous in Norfolk, VA. I had been honored by Steve and Janice Kromer, owners of AGLCA, requesting I present at the Rendezvous.

Attending the event were many new members who were there to see if this was something they could undertake. Also, if they did decide to do it were they capable of being successful? One of the reasons for the Rendezvous is to try to provide answers to questions we all had before making that decision. Keep in mind that many of us also had reservations before we began.

Throughout the event, during the seminars and at the evening parties, I found I was experiencing similar questions and an overwhelmingly common theme seemed to be ANXIETY and FEAR. The desire to undertake the journey was there but in many cases was being suppressed by good old fashion "FEAR OF THE UNKNOWN". "Are we really capable of doing this?"

It was from this awakening I came to see two distinct realizations. I did not recall in all my reading on The Great Loop any attention given to what I now saw as a major concern of those looking for direction and we were just as unsure of a good resource, other than AGLCA, when we began. I decided it was time I did write that book I had been thinking about.

In this book I will not just be telling you about all the wonderful experiences. That will be something you will find out for yourself. *I will try to provide you with some honest guidelines. Allowing you to know that you can do this and you can do it safely and with confidence by doing your research ahead of time and applying just a little common sense, and experience.*

If I could point out to others the things that caused us concern and the issues we ran into, maybe, just maybe I could provide them the freedom of mind to experience the thrill of a lifetime with much less stress.

As I write my goal will be twofold. First, to allow you to see in advance the many satisfactions and anxieties of undertaking an adventure such as this, and trust me; there will be plenty of both. The end result is that hopefully many of you will end up saying, "hey, no problem, we can do that!" If you are one of those, great, give it a try and trust me you will not regret it.

Then again, some of you may find that you have no desire to attempt a journey like this. Not every adventure is meant for everyone. But hopefully reading this story may inspire you to take on another dream rather than let it fade away like so many of us do. Either way my goal is to provide you with a tool to reach out for your dream with minimal ANXIETY and FEAR.

One lesson I learned from this journey is that if you just sit on the aft deck and dream and do nothing about it you may leave a deep emptiness in your life.

You seem to sit there thinking over and over again, what if? The point is that even if we don't succeed in reaching our goals we always have the satisfaction of knowing we tried and that is what I've found becomes most important in later life.

In this book I will be taking you on a day-by-day cruise around the eastern United States and southern Canada as experienced by my wife, Kathy, our faithful dog Deedee and myself. It was a cruise where we came to enjoy and understand a beauty of this continent that cannot be experienced in an automobile, airplane or on foot. I can only hope that in some small way it will show you what wonder awaits you on this beautiful continent and how many wonderful people populate it.

As you follow thru each chapter I will, throughout the book, discuss the "ANXIETY FACTOR" we experienced and overcame during that portion of our journey. Each day it was something new and what seemed at first to be a major problem turned out to be rather minor. It was just another beautiful day on the water. Keep in mind that the "beautiful" part came after we worked our way through it and thought the problem out. Hopefully this book will assist you in eliminating a lot of that stress by providing you with some solutions in advance.

The boat we traveled on was our 1995, Model 3650 Cruisers aft cabin motor yacht named Del Coronado. The boat was 42 feet LOA and powered by twin 454 Crusader fuel injected engines. Carried on board were a10 foot semi-rigid hull Caribe dinghy with a 9.5 h.p. outboard as well as a Yamaha Zuma motor scooter for shore travel.

The crew for our journey was really quite small. It consisted of my wife, Kathy, who may be referred to frequently in the book by her boater rank of Admiral; if you are married I don't have to explain that rank to you. If you are not married just take my word for it.

Also joining us was our First Mate, Deedee. She is our 50 lb. white standard poodle and best friend. The journey would not have been as enjoyable without her company, though there would have been more sleeping room on the Captain's bunk.

We also enjoyed the company of our daughter, Katie and her baby son, Max while traveling down the Gulf coast. Katie helped crew and

FEAR KNOT

Max kept the galley clean by eating everything in sight, a great addition to a great trip.

So let's begin, weigh anchor and keep an eye on our charts as we discover America on America's Great Loop aboard M/V Del Coronado.

Remember as we travel along the way, FEAR KNOT!

Captain Gene Schnagl

THE CREW-Deedee, Katie, Max and Kathy

FEAR KNOT

Del Coronado, 1995 Cruiser's Aft Cabin, 42 LOA

GENE SCHNAGL

CHAPTER 1 – THE BEGINNING

September 13, 2005, the day we've been waiting and preparing for. It seems like it's taken forever. Tomorrow morning we will leave our slip here in Milwaukee Harbor and we honestly don't know when we will pull into it again. I guess we're a little apprehensive but also excited and as ready as we're going to be.

The last few weeks have been incredibly busy. While I've been getting the boat loaded and checking out the equipment Kathy has been getting all the paperwork done. By paperwork I'm referring to such things as forwarding our mail, medications, closing the house down, emergency information, etc. I don't know if we ever realized just how much planning this would take. The preparation itself would fill another book. Bottom line, I think we are ready. It's about 6 AM and I'm sitting on the aft deck with my coffee and laptop. You will find throughout this journey that I do that a lot. I decided to get a little writing in while I had the chance. It's raining pretty hard right now and we're expecting more thunderstorms this afternoon. I'm not worried about it because tomorrow is supposed to be cooler, no rain with some wind out of the northwest. That will be fine as it will give us a following sea on our way south to Chicago, which is always helpful in saving fuel.

Kathy has been trying to get together the little last minute items we forgot. Deedee is sleeping, saving her strength for the strenuous sleeping she'll do on the way and I've just been fixing all the things that I found wrong at the last moment.

I had to design new davits for the dinghy so it would mount behind the motor scooter we are taking with us. I just got those mounted two days ago and everything is working great. I also remembered my golf clubs at the last minute and got them wrapped in heavy plastic and secured on the top of the aft deck by the radar arch. What's Florida without golf clubs?

I then tested the generator and sure enough, the battery was dead so I ran to the store and got a new one right away. Yesterday I got the new Direct TV system working with the new Follow-Me mobile dish antenna. Its working great now but didn't at first until I figured out how to bypass a battery static filter in the antenna/cable wiring system on the boat. It's amazing what you learn to do when you own a boat. To answer your question, no, I still don't know what a "battery static filter" does. To be honest I really don't care, just so it works.

FEAR KNOT

Did I mention that we were prepared for months and all this is happening in the last couple of days? I think all these items were on my many lists but I've killed so many trees making lists I can't find half of them anymore.

Later today we'll head home to close up the house. Our daughter, Katie, will drive us to the marina and we'll be on our way. Tonight we'll spend squaring away the boat and then I'll go over my charts one last time. We'll turn in early tonight and be ready for the morning. Sounds like a plan and we can't wait.

Day 1 - Wednesday, September 14, 2005
We woke very early. I could smell the fresh coffee from the new coffee maker that grinds the beans and makes the coffee all at once. That was a great idea by the Admiral. The coffee is great!

We had thunderstorms most of the night but awoke to clear skies; temp in the mid 70's and winds out of the N/NW at 10-15. Like I said, following seas and clear skies, we're all set. It doesn't get any better than that.

We finally cleared our slip, left McKinley Marina and entered the Milwaukee main harbor. As we cruised south past the city I couldn't help but wonder when we would cruise by it again and what would we see and experience before our return. I guess there was only one way to find out and that was to keep heading south.

Our first stop was at the South Shore Yacht Club at the south end of the harbor. We planned to top off the fuel tanks and pump out the holding tank as our last preparation for the journey. The South Shore Dock Master, Bruce Nason, who always has a big smile on his face, met us at the fuel dock. When I told Bruce where we were headed he wasn't quite sure if we were serious. Then he asked if he could go along. Sorry Bruce, Deedee has your bunk. It wasn't long and we shoved off with the best wishes from Bruce and we headed out of the harbor.

Upon leaving the harbor seawall we had about 1-2 foot seas. That's what we call "flat" water on Lake Michigan. We headed south toward Racine, WI, and it wasn't long before I cruised past the Wind Point Light House just north of Racine Harbor.

We continued south toward Kenosha, WI as the winds continued to build and by the time we reached Waukegan, IL we were experiencing 3-4 ft. seas. I decided to stop at Waukegan harbor to top off the fuel tanks and avoid the high fuel costs in Chicago. By the time we started south again we had seas up to 4-6 ft. This was really starting to be a fun day. Then, when almost within sight of Chicago I heard the Coast Guard put out a small craft warning on the VHF. Wow, thanks gentlemen, I hadn't noticed!

I guess you could say it was a little bumpy heading to Chicago, but Del Coronado handles well in rough water. Deedee was still sleeping under my feet on the bridge so it couldn't be that bad. We had a reservation at Du Sable Marina and made it into our slip with minimal difficulty. Kathy and Deedee immediately headed to shore while I secured the boat. Deedee was a little unsteady walking but got her land legs back quickly and enjoyed the grass.

Now you can't go to Chicago without spending a couple of days enjoying the city. There is just so much to see and do. Besides, the weather was really bad and we thought we would wait it out. The problem was the forecasts didn't show any improvement for a least a few days.

We did experience one little incident on our second day in Chicago. Kathy was taking Deedee ashore before we turned in for the night. The wind was really howling and it was very dark. The two of them were going off the swim platform onto a floating dock and I was up above on the aft deck. Suddenly I heard Kathy yell, but as I looked down I couldn't see her on the dock. It wasn't until I ran down the aft steps to the swim platform that I could see Kathy hanging in the water between the boat and the dock with one arm over the dock line and holding onto Deedee with the other. I grabbed the dog and her and yanked them both up on the dock. Besides cold and wet, Kathy took some heavy bruising under the arm and along the ribs, but everyone was ok. Sure enough, as they stepped to the dock a gust of wind caught the boat and yanked them and in they went. You can never be too careful around boats. Accidents can happen. I guess it was another example of lines stretching when wet and needing to be reset.

After getting everyone safely aboard it was time to call it a night and get some rest. Tomorrow morning we'll be heading through the first lock into the Chicago River. The weather just kept getting colder and wetter and the wind kept gaining speed. We can only hope for some improvement by morning.

ANXIETY FACTOR – CAN I REALLY DO THIS?

I'm going to discuss the two major CAUSES FOR CONCERN that I believe you may experience before you even begin this voyage. I hope I can explain them clearly enough for you to understand the importance for us.

First, let me provide you with a little background on myself. I've always been a "big" guy, 6' 2" and 250 plus pounds. I played football, hockey and baseball as a kid. I was a certified Scuba diver when I was 15 and a Judo Instructor at age 16. I am a U.S. Army Veteran and spent 27 years in law enforcement. I was a Patrolman, Detective Sergeant, Undercover Narcotics Agent, S.W.A.T. Team Negotiator, Organized Crime Task Force Investigator, Homicide/Major Crimes Investigator and Polygraph Examiner. I was Security Director for three states for a national bank after retiring from law enforcement. Then I retired again and went into boating to begin enjoying life to the fullest.

Now with all that behind me I wasn't afraid of too much, at least that's what I showed on the outside to those who knew me. I want you to know that I was somewhat scared before I pulled away from the dock to start this trip. I thought I was taking a big risk and I wasn't too sure about it. Yet, with all that concern I never took the time to discuss that fear with Kathy. Call it fear or call it anxiety, the issue is that I never shared it with the one person that was most important for the success of the trip, the person I was placing at the same risk level as myself.

I suppose I was so nervous because in all that macho past I usually just had to worry about myself and sometimes a partner who was as big as me and probably twice as tough.

Now I was embarking on a decision that not only involved me but Kathy as well. A decision that was going to change our lifestyle and, let's be honest, it was going to cost us some money as well. Was I asking her to do this for us or was it just for me?

Some of you may respond by saying, that's not me. I know I can handle all this and those thoughts don't bother me at all. More power to you gentlemen, I envy you! Yet, as I write this I wish someone would have vocalized these thoughts to me before I left on the trip as I wouldn't have worried about it as much. If they had, I would have known that I wasn't the only one who had the doubts about my own abilities and the weeks and months of unknowns ahead of me.

Like many of my friends, we have all boated for years. The problem is we have always been boating on the same waters year after year. I was now going to go through about 146 locks with monster tow boats and barges. I would be going into debris clogged rivers and swamps and into tidal waters which I knew nothing about. The list goes on and on and I didn't really know what I would be facing. All I knew is that this was something I truly wanted to do and I had to make sure that we didn't get hurt along the way.

In hindsight I wish I would have spent time with the AGLCA before we left, to learn more about what I was headed into. Time spent discussing my concerns with experienced boaters who had already been where I was headed. I know that if I had, I would have done the one thing I should have done first and that was to let Kathy know that I had some fear and concern but I was confident we could overcome any problems together. I think that pre-discussion would have made me more comfortable as we started the engines that first morning.

Since completing The Great Loop, Kathy and I have discussed this issue and she agrees she would have been much more comfortable had I shared my concerns with her before we set out. After all, she reminded me, her job is to take care of me as well as mine is to take care of her.

I feel it is important that you have these discussions ahead of time and understand that you both have doubts and concerns over what is ahead. I would highly recommend that you put those thoughts and reservations on the table before you for discussion and be open with each other about them.

I believe that in the end you will both find that you will be there for each other and experience everyday how, that together; you become stronger and stronger in your efforts to reach your goal. Men, don't be afraid to share your thoughts! Remember, the women share them willingly with us every day of our lives!

ANXIETY FACTOR – WILL I BE ABLE TO ENDURE THESE LIMITED CONDITIONS FOR SUCH AN EXTENDED PERIOD OF TIME?

Let me point out a few things that "The Admiral" didn't mention to me before we started, but had concerned her a lot.

We men tend to be concerned about men things, right? Things like, do they have beer in Florida? Can you get pizza in North Carolina? There are a lot of important things like that we are concerned about but don't discuss with our wives.

What we fail to think about many times are the very special issues that our spouses are concerned with. Things like, where can I get my nails done? How often will I get to see the grandchildren? Will we stay where I can get my hair done? Will there be other gals to talk to? The list goes on, but it is a very important list and they are deeply concerned about those questions.

Men can go weeks without shaving and think the beard is cool looking. Just go on a fishing or hunting trip with a group of guys and you know what I'm talking about. Ladies, on the other hand, just don't think like that. They need to feel comfortable and clean which means you need to discuss that ANXIETY with them before you leave on your trip. She will need to know that you understand, come the end of a long day on the water, that she will want to get cleaned up and relax. She will need time to be a woman and she will need to know she is not going to get an argument from you every day about it. You are going to be on a small boat for a long time together and you can make it a very enjoyable time just by remembering why you became a couple in the first place. Anchoring out every night can save money but spending an occasional night at a marina can be a blessing for the crew. Getting cleaned up and going out to dinner, even at McDonalds, can be a great stress reliever.

FEAR KNOT

Dockmaster Bruce Nason at the South Shore Yacht Club sending us off

Goodbye to Milwaukee, Wisconsin

DuSable Marina, Chicago, Illinois

GENE SCHNAGL

The Ship's Office

Chicago Harbor waves are up

Fall in, you get a bath

FEAR KNOT

Our first lock, Chicago

Downtown Chicago

Chicago Amtrak Bridge

GENE SCHNAGL

CHAPTER 2 – THE RIVER DILEMMA

Day 3 – We woke to more rain but still screaming wind. It really made us wonder if we should wait another day. The plan is to try to get through the lock and into the rivers and out of the heavy wind. We'll see how it goes. I do know one thing, it can't be any worse than out here on the lake.

It was fun getting out of the slip and into the inner Chicago harbor with the flat line winds out of the north. Just in the harbor we had 3-4 ft. waves and then it was a little tricky getting into the first lock. We got tied up to the starboard lock wall, but had a rough time holding there. It probably would have been easier to tie port but the lockmaster told us to stay starboard and, in hindsight, he was right. I would have never gotten off the port wall in the wind. The winds were so strong they tore the aft deck canvas out of the track and it was flapping in the wind. I just had to leave it and hope it held until we got into the river. This was our first lock ever and Kathy came through like a champ. Sore ribs and arm and fighting terrible winds she held the boat to the lock wall forward while I held us aft so we could make it through. I think I married the right crewmember.

The river was much calmer, just as we had hoped. I repaired the canvas and we began cruising our way through the city of Chicago. It was fantastic traveling through such a massive urban area with the traffic all around and no traffic problems for us. After a short distance Kathy took the helm and I climbed up on top by the radar arch to lower the TV dish to make sure we made it under the low Chicago bridges ahead. What a Captain I am, I got it lowered and Kathy took us under the bridges. Crack! Crack! It seems that the great Captain lowered the dish, but forgot about the VHF and Loran antennas, which were both now about 18 inches shorter. Are we having fun or what? I guess we are because I can't get the Admiral to stop laughing. It must be a girl thing because I don't see what's so funny. This is beginning to sound like a Three Stooges movie and we've just gotten started.

Well, we're on the river and heading south and it is quiet now that the laughter has died down. Even heavy industry and shipping has a beauty about it if you just look at it from the water instead of the street. I guess being on the water allows you to view areas seen every day, from a new perspective. It wasn't long and we approached the Amtrak Bridge which allows only a 16 foot clearance. I attempted to contact the bridge attendant by radio to request a bridge opening. No answer! Now, having been made aware ahead of time to possibly expect this type of response I tried to contact the attendant by cell phone. No answer! After numerous horn attempts, radio calls, cell calls, etc. I still got no response. Now keep in mind that the whole time I was trying to hold position in the center of the river with boats piling up behind me who were also trying to contact the attendant. I should also note, that at no time during this experience did a train cross over the bridge.

I decided it was time to try a different approach to the problem. In anticipation, I had, in preparation for the trip, obtained the personal cell phone number for the Amtrak Railroad Superintendent in Chicago. Kathy called him and in a very "lady like" manner expressed our displeasure. Very quickly the bridge went up and as we passed underneath I noticed a guy standing by the bridge operations shack with a very nasty look on his face. I could only assume that he didn't like me or that he had a bad case of gas. Well, either way, we were on our way again.

After the bridge delay we were unable to make it to the next lock until around 4:00pm. The lock is located at Lockport, IL. Waiting for an opening were two tows with barges standing by to lock through, one up bound and one down bound. One had eight barges and one had fifteen barges.

Tows with lots of barges don't fit into locks as a unit. They are required to perform what is known as a "CUT." The lock is opened and the tow will push in as many barges that will fit. The barges are then cut loose and the tow with the remaining barges backs out. The lock lifts the barges and then shoves them out the other end and ties them to a wall. They then lower the lock again, open it and the tow with the remainder of the barges enter and the procedure is repeated. The unit is then hooked back together and off they go.

The problem is that a process like this can take up to three to four hours and commercial traffic is a priority before recreational boaters. Knowing this procedure we knew we wouldn't get through until late so I contacted the lockmaster by radio and requested permission to tie up to the lock wall for the night. He advised us to enjoy the evening and we tied up for the night. I lifted Deedee up on the lock wall and Kathy took her for a walk while I prepared a couple of cocktails for us. We relaxed and enjoyed the sunset and spent a quiet night at the lock. After a stressful day it made for a very relaxing evening and we really were enjoying ourselves despite the delays.

Day 4 – In the morning we awoke to fog so heavy we couldn't see the lock gate just ahead of us. We decided to wait until it burned off and around 8:00 am I contacted the lockmaster and he told us to come on in. We locked down about 40 ft. and continued on our journey south.

We made two more locks that day, Brandon Lock and Dresden Lock. We accomplished both of them before noon and were moving right along. It was sunny, warm and life was good.

At about 1:30 P.M. we arrived at the last lock I wanted to make that day, the Marseilles lock just north of Starved Rock Marina where we had made a reservation to spend the evening. I gained some more knowledge about locking at this location. Upon arriving, there was a tow with barges waiting to lock down bound. He had to make a cut and the first half of barges had red flags on them. That meant they contained hazardous cargo and no vessel can be in the lock with them. They went through and the last barges and tow entered. The lockmaster told me I could slide in with the remaining tow and barges if I wanted to, as we had been waiting about two hours and there were no hazardous materials with this part of the unit. This is where my locking knowledge data base took a surge and I learned a new locking lesson.

We were tied up on the port wall behind the tow when during the locking down process something came loose on the barges and the Tow Captain had to adjust his position in the lock. Keep in mind at this point that towboats have huge engines and very large propellers. As the Captain started adjusting inside the lock everything started moving behind the tow, and I do mean everything. As our boat was the only thing behind the tow except the lock door it got pretty wild. I contacted the tow captain on the radio and he immediately shut down and apologized, having forgotten I was in there with him. There was no damage, but my eyes were a lot bigger and we had to stop Deedee from abandoning ship. Just a note, we didn't go into any more locks with tows after this date no matter how long we had to wait. Upon leaving the lock I passed the tow and barges with a friendly wave from the tow captain and crew as we proceeded south to Starved Rock Marina.

Now we had reached the highlight of our Great Loop adventure. As we were cruising slowly along, enjoying the scenery, I suddenly noticed the rpm on the starboard engine just drop to nothing and I had no power in that engine. I immediately shut the engine down and decided we would simply have to limp our way for a few miles to the marina on one engine until I could determine exactly what the problem was. I was able to maneuver into a slip and we spent the night wondering what lay in store for us the next day. It just didn't seem like a great start to a yearlong journey. This happened on a Saturday and on Sunday morning we found that the repair shop would not be open until Monday. We decided to make the best of it and I unloaded the motor scooter and we went exploring. We actually had a great weekend and enjoyed our time ashore. Riding through the back country roads is really a ball on a motor scooter. It's amazing what you find to see and do. I guess the old adage is true, when given lemons you might as well make lemonade.

Monday morning arrived and the mechanic from Starved Rock Marina came to the boat early. After a period of time examining the starboard engine we received the bad news. Our engine had blown and we would require the installation of a new engine. This is definitely news that no boat owner wants to hear. We met with the service manager and tried to figure out what had happened and what we would do now.

Lucky for us, Starved Rock Marina is a full service marina and could handle the problem for us. They were able to locate a new engine in Missouri and would send a crew overnight to pick it up. In the morning we would begin the process of removing the old engine so we would be ready when the new engine arrived. Now came all the fun.

First, I moved the boat to their boat ramp and backed it in, which is always fun on one engine. Then a hoist was constructed in our main cabin over the engine compartment which I kept bumping my head on, so we wrapped it in old carpet fragments. It was either that or continuing to dent my already balding head. The critical part came in figuring out how to get a small crane boom into the main cabin to lift the engine out of the boat. We were very fortunate that Cruiser's Yachts put some thought into their designs. On some aft cabin vessels the entire upper deck has to be lifted off to remove engines. We were fortunate as we found that we could lift the aft deck side curtains and extend the boom right through the main cabin hatch to the hoist. After removing engine parts down to the main engine block they were able to hoist the engine up and then straight out through the hatch (our 'now in pieces' aft door) and we were ready for the new engine.

The next day the new engine arrived and they began the process of getting us back together. Then all we had left to do was take her out for sea trials.

I imagine at this point you might be asking, what caused all this trouble in the first place, right? Let me try to explain that. It seems that the #2 and #4 spark plugs had backed out of the block until #4 caused a detonation and blew a one inch hole through that cylinder. The mechanic believed that the plugs did not have the proper torque and that caused them to back out. This now inspires the question, who pays for all this?

Normally insurance would not cover something like this, as it is considered owner error. In this case, however, I had documented the work done and then took digital photos of all the work and the internal damage to the engine. Also, the week prior to our departure I had a certified mechanic go over the engines and service them. The service included new belts, spark plugs, oil & water filters, etc. I had copies of all the bills with me in our ships book. I also had the Starved Rock Marine Service Department keep all removed parts stored in a secure place until our insurance company had a chance to review them. Kathy then contacted our insurance company and explained our problem. They immediately assigned an investigator out of Chicago who then contacted me by phone. To save time I offered to fax him all the documents and email all the photos directly to him. I did this and shortly he called me back and said with the information I provided he would ok payment to us and they would seek restitution with our mechanic's insurance company. The check was cut immediately and sent to Starved Rock for payment, minus the deductable. This was a very good day. All I can say is, like any good Captain, document, document, and document.

The following day we took the boat out for sea trials and everything was great. We were now prepared to continue on our journey and it had only cost us five days. I can't say enough about the staff at Starved Rock Marina and would recommend the harbor as a must stop on The Loop.

ANXIETY FACTOR – ARE WE GOING TO BE ABLE TO MAKE IT THROUGH ALL THOSE LOCKS?

I'll admit that the first lock can be kind of intimidating, but in all honesty they are actually fairly easy to get into and out of. Just remember to do a little study before you head out. Talk to experienced boaters before hand and become aware of some of the locking dos and don'ts.

When locking, Captains, you have to remember that your job is to maneuver that vessel into position for your deckhand to get that lock wall tie off. Once the tie is made then it's your job to assist the deckhand in securing the vessel. The biggest problem in locking seems to occur when the Captain and deckhand start yelling at each other and arguing about what to do, when to do it and who is in charge. Don't worry, we've all been there and it does get much easier with time and practice.

Once I realized that Kathy really knew more about getting that boat secured than I did and that I knew more about maneuvering than she did, we resolved our differences. I would get the boat in position and then she was in charge to get it secured. If she said go forward, go back, hold it right there, I just did it and didn't ask her why. The problems disappeared and life was good again.

Also, remember that the Lock Master is there to assist you and if you just listen to him or her and pay attention, they will get you in just fine. They do this for a living and meet hundreds of boaters every day. Ask your questions before the problems occur and don't be embarrassed. They love to help and avoid problems. It's kind of like being back in school. The person behind you has the same question, but is also embarrassed to ask. Do it first and help everyone out.

ANXIETY FACTOR – WHAT IF WE HAVE A MAJOR PROBLEM WITH THE BOAT?

We all know that this can happen, after all, it is a boat and all boats have mechanical problems now and then. Kathy and I knew starting out that there are things that can go wrong big time. In our case we tried to anticipate everything, but that honestly never quite works out the way you want it to. It is a sure thing that something is going to go wrong sooner or later.

By having our engines completely gone over just before we left was the best thing I could have done. Documenting all the work was even more important. When the engine did blow, I was able to show that it wasn't through my carelessness that it occurred. I had documented all the work I had done and I had the documentation with me. I also knew who I needed to contact as we had all our insurance information with us.

Should we not have been prepared for a problem we would have had a very large out of pocket expense just a few days into our trip and we may have been delayed for an extended period of time. As it was, we were able to keep our personal cost to a minimum and be back on the water in a few days.

The answer is that problems are going to occur so just don't worry about them. Be prepared ahead of time and have all the information you will need available and you will make big problems into little ones. Besides, we now know that Starved Rock Marina is as good a Marina as they say they are!

FEAR KNOT

PHOTOS

Installing the new engine

An expensive blown piston

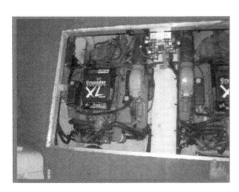

New engine, ready to go

Deedee ready to go

Holding position for a train crossing

Free floating an Illinois River lock

FEAR KNOT

Holding to enter Lockport lock

Arriving at Peoria, Illinois

A beautiful Illinois River sunset

GENE SCHNAGL

CHAPTER 3 – SOUTHBOUND ON THE ILLINOIS RIVER

Today is Friday, September 23, 2005 and we've been on the water just eleven days. We have learned how to "lock", we have a new engine and the sun is shining. It's time we started heading south to warmer weather.

After clearing Starved Rock Marina we almost immediately entered Starved Rock Lock and locked through with only one other vessel. This was going to be our only lock today, as we planned on heading to Peoria, IL. and spend the night at Eastport Marina. We did have to make a fuel stop at a small marina on the way and ended up maneuvering in some very tight quarters, but made it without a problem. This is really the difficulty of having gas engines rather than diesel. You have to plot your fuel stops very carefully, as marine gas is not as plentiful as diesel on the rivers. It's a good idea to consider this in advance to avoid problems.

Eastport Marina was a great stop. We had dinner with some fellow boaters we met and called it an early evening. We had to turn down an invitation for a party at the yacht club that following evening as we had to get moving, but it would have been fun and the invitation was very thoughtful.

Our first lock today was Peoria Lock and Dam. There was no other traffic and the wind was dead calm. I was surprised when the lockmaster told me that if I wanted I could just free float the lock. This is a little unusual as most always you will be required to tie up in a lock. In this case I just got the boat in the center of the lock and as we were going down we just floated free. Kathy thought that all locks should be done that way but I'm afraid she was out of luck.

Our goal today is to try to make up for some of the time we lost with the engine repair. We hope to make it to Joe Wheeler State Park in Alabama for the America's Great Loop Cruisers' Association Rendezvous. I've plotted out our next fuel stop so we'll keep the speed up a little bit and cruise on down the river. My plans today are a little ambitious as I'm going to try and make it the 164 miles down the Illinois River to the Mississippi River and then 18 miles to Alton, IL on the Mississippi. We'll just have to see how things go. There are plenty of anchorages along the way but we are trying to make up the time and also we prefer to stay at marinas when we can rather than anchor out. You can imagine that Deedee prefers that, which is really our reason for doing it. What we don't do for our kids and pets. We made good time and arrived at our fuel stop. Now we received another surprise. It seems our fuel stop consisted of two large rusted fuel tanks setting on a small barge in a cutout in the bank of the river. The cutout wasn't much wider than our boat so with the strong river current I was going to have to try and power us in a little so we didn't slide by and into the down bound bank. Kathy called the marina office by cell and a fellow came out and yelled to me that there was only about three feet of water about ten feet past the end of the fuel barge. Since I draw three and one half feet the math didn't quite compute. I really needed the fuel so I told him I would ground the bow and we would drag the fuel hoses aft to fill.

After putting the bow aground we were alongside the barge, but only the front half of the boat. That meant that when Kathy went to take Deedee ashore I had to lower her by hand to the barge and then hand Deedee down to her. (Fig. 18)

Our tanks hold 300 gallons so I wanted to put about 200 gallons in to top off. After filling the port tank I transferred the hose to the starboard tank but after about 20 gallons the pump shut down and the guy told me he was sorry that they were out of fuel. Just Great! Not only did I not get enough fuel but I got the last of the fuel in the tank. This was what you never wanted to happen as the fuel could have a lot of water in it which could be a real problem. I added some Heat fuel additive to the fuel tanks just to be on the safe side. I then had to power us off the bottom and back into the river and we continued south. I'm not sure about this, but I thought I could hear "dueling banjos" music playing in the woods as we cleared the shore. It was probably just my imagination. I have to admit, it was an interesting stop.

I knew today was going to be another one of those days when after a few miles I came around an S curve in the river and had to come to a complete stop. There, sideways in the river, was a tow with a load of barges. The current was very strong and the tow Captain had somehow lost control of the barges and was jammed bank to bank. I notified the Captain of the tow by radio that I would hold position while he tried to maneuver his way free.

After about a half hour the Captain managed to power the tow clear of the starboard down bound bank. As he did so he told me to try and slip through behind him and he would cut his engines down while I did it. Everything worked fine and we were able to make it by without problem and we continued on our way. I guess even the pros have problems on the water. These towboat captains are a great group of guys and gals, if you just remember to work with them you will be much better off on the water.

We finally arrived at Beardstown, IL where we would have to decide to continue on to Alton, IL or not. It would make for a very long day but we decided to commit and on we went. It wasn't long and we arrived at the LaGrange Lock. We were lucky again and there was no other river traffic and the lock master told us we could free float again. Kathy was really starting to enjoy this locking stuff as long as we could continue to free float. The remainder of the day was pretty quiet and we just continued southbound making very good time.

Now comes the, "Do as I say, Not as I do" part. About 20 miles short of the Mississippi the sun set and we were headed into darkness on the rivers. I strongly urge all of you not to run the rivers after dark unless you really have to. In strange waters with barges and tows, wing dams, strong currents, shoals, etc., it is no time to be out there if you can avoid it. With that being said, I didn't follow my own advice and we continued on our way but much more cautious in our attempt to make it to Alton, IL before calling it a day. If we made it to Alton it would put us back on schedule to make the AGLCA rendezvous on time.

ANXIETY FACTOR – WHAT KIND OF BOAT WILL WE NEED FOR THE LOOP?

Everyone worries that they don't have the right boat for The Loop. Do we want a big one or a small one, a powerboat or a sailboat, gas or diesel?

There is no set answer to the question about which boat to take. That is going to be up to you and your personal likes and comfort levels. My only comments on this issue are the following:

Kathy and I did The Loop in a large power boat with gas engines. It worked well and we had a great trip. However, using gas engines means higher fuel costs and consumption and you do need a lot of range for a cruise like this. Just on the Mississippi you will need to be able to make it from Hoppie's Marina all the way to the Kentucky Lock and Dam before you will be able to find gas for a refuel. That is a distance of around 230 miles. That will put you way outside the one third, one third, one third rule. The Rule states that you use one third of the fuel for the trip out, one third of the fuel for the trip back and one third is kept in reserve for emergencies.

Knowing your fuel consumption rate and range is a priority safety rule for America's Great Loop.

I personally prefer a trawler style boat. They tend to have the fuel range and economy required as well as the size and comfort level for this type of cruise, but again, that is just my personal preference.

No matter what boat you take just be sure to plan your distances well and know where your fuel stops are located so you don't have to stretch your fuel needs outside safety limits.

ANXIETY FACTOR – WHAT IF WE HAVE TO TRAVEL AT NIGHT?

I would recommend very strongly that you not travel at night unless you absolutely cannot avoid it. The reasons are many but I will cover just a few to show you why.

On open waters such as The Gulf you are normally cruising far enough off shore that you cannot see any shore lights at all. The only lights you will see are your instruments and running lights. Constant position awareness is a must, as well as an alert topside crew. The Gulf coasts are shallow and shoaling is common all along the coasts.

Rivers present an entirely different set of problems for night running. The channels are very narrow and constantly changing from one side of the river to the other. Wing dams are prevalent and constant course awareness must be maintained. The other big factor is the barge traffic which runs 24/7.

Should you have to run at night do not fear it but be sure you understand the use of your instruments and that they are properly functioning. You will be using them constantly. Also have your crew members on deck assisting you in observing the surrounding waters for marker buoys, other vessels, etc. Take it slow and take it easy and you should be just fine.

Many boaters travel at night, but most of them know the waters they are on well and have traveled them many times in the past. Remember, even the professional captains on the tows like to bank the tows for the night and just travel by day. You will be traveling waters that you do not know so it is just good common sense to stick to the daylight hours.

Eliminating the <u>ANXIETY FACTOR</u> is rather easy in this regard. Just try not to put yourself in a time commitment where you must be somewhere at a specific time or date. You are on a cruise and it is designed to stop and smell the roses, so take advantage of it.

GENE SCHNAGL

CHAPTER 4 – THE MIGHTY MISSISSIPPI

We continued on into the darkness with the chart plotter, radar, spot light and Kathy with the binoculars and we proceeded to make our way through all the obstacles. We were on the Mississippi now and the channels get very tricky. You find yourself going from the port bank and then all the way across to the starboard bank and back again many times just to maintain the center of the channel. You must stay in the channels or you will be hard aground or worse, so extreme caution is needed, especially in the dark. As we continued on, the weather took another turn and it started to rain so hard we could hardly see the bow and I was relying almost completely on my instruments.

As we continued south in the distance we could finally see the glow of the lights from the Alton Riverboat Casinos and the bridge over the river, so we knew our night was coming to a close.

We finally made it into our slip at the Alton Marina about 9:30pm. We had covered 178 miles on the water that day and were exhausted. As tired as we were, we decided to take the time to clean up the boat and take hot showers on board before calling it a night. Sleep is going to come easy, believe me. Oh, almost forgot, Deedee hit the shore and was totally in heaven. I think she had a long day also. Have you ever seen a dog smile and sigh? Interesting!

Well, I was right, we had a great night's sleep. Probably because it poured rain all night and it was still pouring come daylight. With the rain and the high humidity everything felt damp. All we can do is hope we can dry out soon.

ANXIETY FACTOR – HOW MANY MILES SHOULD WE TRY TO COVER IN A DAY?

Cruising can be very tiring for the Captain and crew. Hours of maintaining alertness and concentration can take its toll. The more hours cruising, the more tired the crew gets, the better the chances of something going wrong.

Try to limit yourself to short cruising days. You don't have to hit the water before sunup, especially on the rivers. Early morning fog is very common on the rivers and yet many boats try to head out right away to be the first in the locks. The problem is the tows have spent the night sleeping in the locks and they are not heading out until the fog lifts. Many times I have heard the radio chatter of boats playing bumper tag in the fog while I sat at the slip drinking my coffee. What I would do was be sure I had the phone numbers for all the locks with me on board. When I got up in the morning I would call the lock master by phone and ask when he thought he might be opening. Many times he told me not until the fog lifts. I would then ask if he could give a horn blast when he planned on opening and then I would head out. I never had one disagree and it saved us a lot of headaches.

FEAR KNOT

Ending the day early also offers you a better chance of locating a good slip or anchorage. You can relax, clean up the boat and yourselves and plan for the next day. Hitting the sack early is always a pleasure on the water where sleep comes easy.

The day was going to be a short run of about 45 miles south to the best stop on the Mississippi River, Hoppie's Marina. With such a short run we decided to treat ourselves before we left. We hopped on the Marina shuttle and headed to the River Boat Casino for a breakfast buffet. As we had to wait for the buffet to open we decided to play a couple of slots. As usual we lost. Wait, did I just say we lost? Actually I lost $20 but Kathy won $29 so "we" came out ahead. The end result was that Kathy advised me to stick to navigation and she would handle the gambling. She got no argument from me and the buffet was great, so all ended well.

After returning to the marina we slipped the lines and continued down the river in the rain. The wind picked up as well, so visibility became a concern, but we did just fine.

On the Mississippi we would only have two locks to work through and we arrived at the first, Lock 26. As there was no traffic, the lockmaster told me to go ahead and free float again if I wanted. As we got centered in the cell the lockmaster contacted me by radio and advised that one other pleasure craft was coming so we would wait a couple of minutes for him and we could both free float. Shortly the other boat arrived and we had an easy lock through and continued south.

The other boat we locked through with was out of Minnetonka, MN and as we were both headed to Hoppie's Marina we decided to stick together as we cruised. It seems to make the journey much more pleasant sometimes when cruising with another boat. In this case it turned out to not only be pleasant, but very helpful for our traveling companions.

We hadn't gone very far when the rain started to come down even harder, which really didn't seem possible. To add to it, the fog settled in and it was going to be travel by instruments only for awhile. As I had the chart plotter and the radar and the other boat didn't have the instrumentation, they slid in behind me and we inched our way south. I stayed in radio contact with the tow captains around us and we continued without incident. During this time Kathy was also following the paper charts and marking off the channel buoy numbers as we passed them. We had made it a policy that she would always double check our position in heavy fog or limited visibility situations. This may seem redundant, but I do believe it might have kept us out of some serious problems during our journey where buoys had been knocked out of position or were gone altogether.

ANXIETY FACTOR – SHOULD I HAVE PAPER CHARTS ON BOARD EVEN IF I HAVE ALL THE ELECTRONICS?

How many times have I heard, "I don't need any paper charts, I have state of the art electronics"? I guess, just about as many times as I've heard, "I blew a fuse and lost my instruments. We were stuck and I didn't know what to do".

Having paper charts is not required with electronics except on ships, but it really is a good habit to get in to. Kathy and I carried a total of 93 lbs of paper charts on board. Paper charts covering every body of water we would pass through. In heavy fog situations Kathy would check off the markers as I located them. What was interesting is that occasionally while I was concentrating on maneuvering she would note on the chart the marker that I just passed didn't seem to be in the right place. In checking, I found that the marker had probably been pulled out of place by a barge and I was able to make the proper course changes to allow for it.

Also, if that fuse blows, you are still able to navigate until you can get repairs made. Another major problem made easy by planning ahead.

We finally made it to Lock 27 and both boats were allowed to free float again. The wind had picked up somewhat, but we were both able to hold position and the lock was incident free. A short time later the rain let up, the wind died down and the sun came out. Maybe this was going to be a not such a bad day after all.

It wasn't long and we reached our destination, the famous Hoppie's Marina. Now why, you may ask, is this marina famous? Well, I'll tell you why. Hoppie and his wife, Fern, are legends among boaters on the Mississippi River. Their marina is the last stop before you hit the fork of the Mississippi and the Ohio rivers. That makes it a MUST STOP for AGLCA boaters. They are also the very best source of information regarding river conditions that boaters will find. You just aren't going to find more friendly and knowledgeable people regarding the rivers to assist you.

As you approach Hoppie's marina you will see that it consists of a long steel dock along the down bound starboard bank of the Mississippi river. It is here that you will really learn one of the major rules of river docking. As the current along the Mississippi river can be extremely fast at times, you never want to come into a dock "down bound". If you do this you will find that you have no control over your boat due to the current and you'll probably meet the boat in front of you head on and it will hurt. Always turn your vessel and approach the dock "up bound". This will allow you to use the current to help control your boat and you will be able to ease it into the dock just fine. Besides, if you come at the dock at Hoppie's the wrong way you will hear about it from Hoppie or Fern so heed my advice. Hoppie and Fern are not afraid to express their feelings.

It can get a little bumpy at this dock, as the tows go by 24/7 and the wakes rock your boat a little, but you'll get used to it. Just make sure your lines are snug.

ANXIETY FACTOR – HOW WOULD WE FIND OUT IF THERE ARE PROBLEMS AHEAD OF US?

The AGLCA is your number one answer, as well as your Waterway Guides, which everyone should have on board. Also the AGLCA website allows you to communicate with other Loopers and keep abreast of changes such as lock closures, etc.

You will find that Local Knowledge is also a valuable resource. Fern and Hoppie are a prime example. Just remember that you have to decide if the "local knowledge" is in fact knowledgeable. Just because the fellow is sitting there on the dock or boat doesn't mean that he is local or that he knows anything about boating. You may want to ask a few questions to see if he knows what he is talking about before following his advice.

I've had Loopers tell me that they don't trust local knowledge because they received bad information once. In a case like this I don't know if the local gave the wrong information or if the Looper didn't ask the right questions. Just apply the number one boating tool, common sense, and you will usually come out ok.

After our traveling companions and we were tied up, we relaxed in the dockside boater's lounge area with other boaters for the evening. Another boating day behind us and bad weather or not, I love the life on the water. Naturally it started raining again, but the boater's lounge is sheltered and we weren't delayed in sharing a drink and experiences of the day with our new found friends.

Come morning it had finally stopped raining and was just gloomy and overcast. After breakfast we took the time to fuel up and then continued south on the Mississippi river. Be sure to fuel up at Hoppie's if you have gas engines. If you have diesel engines the next fuel stop is about 60 miles south at Cape Girardeau, Missouri. If you have gas engines you need to do some planning before departing Hoppie's. You will need the range to get from Hoppie's to the Kentucky Dam at the Ohio and Tennessee River junction, a distance of about 230 miles, as Cape Girardeau no longer has gas but diesel fuel only. A lot of boaters purchase 6 gal. fuel cans to carry onboard so they can refuel themselves while on the way. You may also want to check with AGLCA resources regarding contacting a fuel truck for a delivery at a specific location for multiple boats. Many truckers have a minimum order that they will deliver, so check before you purchase. Just make sure you have a sufficient supply to reach your destination and don't leave yourself in harm's way or get stranded in the middle of nowhere.

After fueling we started south with our next destination being Cape Girardeau, MO. Our Buddy Boat was still with us and we had a pleasant trip down river. Before arriving at Cape Girardeau I called the fuel company by cell to arrange for them to meet us at their dock. The owner's name is Charlie Brown, honest! Charlie brought a tanker truck down to the bank above his fuel dock on the river and the fuel was pumped from the truck to the boat. It worked great. Just remember that this service for gas is no longer provided, but was at the time we passed through.

There is one small problem here if you have a big boat. The fuel dock is very short, in our case only about 10 ft. longer than our boat. The current is also very strong and the tow wakes make it a little bumpy so be careful when docking and fueling.

ANXIETY FACTOR – HOW DO WE KNOW WHERE THERE ARE SAFE PLACES TO ANCHOR?

Your Waterway guides such as Skipper Bob's Publications are your number one resource to answer this question. They research these sites and keep on top of any changes that may occur. Use of this resource will give you the information you will need and provide you with safe, comfortable anchorages.

After both boats were fueled we headed south a short distance to the Little Diversion Channel. This is a great spot to anchor for the night before heading down to the Ohio River in the morning. The only issue is that you must be very careful when entering the channel from the Mississippi river.   Remember the fast current we talked about? Be ready for it when you try to make the turn into the channel. The best bet here is to go past the entry which will be on your down bound starboard side. Then turn around and approach up bound to use that current to help control your vessel. This will keep you from getting pushed into the large rocks along the south shoreline of the entry.

<u>*ANXIETY FACTOR*</u> *– DOES THE CURRENT ON THE RIVERS CAUSE YOU ANY PROBLEMS?*

If you normally boat the Great Lakes you will probably not have experienced a lot of current. On the major rivers such as the Mississippi and the Ohio you will need to become accustomed to the strong currents and the eddy pools they can cause.

Currents on the rivers and tidal currents can pull your boat out of channels and into trouble areas if you are not paying attention and making adjustments in a timely manner. Be alert and be ready should this happen.

FEAR KNOT

When docking or turning into side channels off the rivers, never approach the dock or channel from a down bound direction. This means that you never approach with the current pushing you from behind. Always go past the point you want to dock or the entrance to the channel and approach in an up bound direction. Now you are using the current to help control your boat.

Once in the channel, it is easy going but somewhat narrow and shallow. Some of the larger vessels may even experience a little difficulty turning around so be a little cautious. You will only be able to proceed a few hundred yards in until you reach a small bridge which will stop your progress. Most of the boats in here will usually raft up with bow and stern anchors to keep the boats from swinging into the banks. Once you are anchored you will find yourself secure in a protected area.

For us, I anchored bow and stern and decided to raft our companion boat to us, as we had better ground tackle. The gals then decided they should take the dogs back to the fuel dock for a walk so **Kathy and Deedee** went with our companions on their boat and headed back upstream to Cape Girardeau. As I was now alone I broke out the fishing rod, a cold beer and did some fishing off the stern. I caught one large catfish, but decided to catch and release.

A local fisherman in a bass boat came by and we started talking so I asked him to join me for a beer which he immediately accepted. We got to talking about all the Asian carp and he related to me how a couple of weeks earlier he and his buddy tangled with one of them. It seems that they were fishing just at the entrance to Little Diversion Channel. He was seated in the back of the boat and his pal was in the bow. As the current is so strong in that area he revved the motor a little to maintain a safe distance from the rocky shoreline. As he did this he asked his pal a question, but his pal didn't answer so he looked forward and saw that his pal was gone. At that moment he noticed his pal pop up to the surface of the water going downstream away from the boat in the current. After recovering his friend he found out that as he revved the motor an Asian Carp had jumped and hit his pal and knocked him overboard. Nobody was hurt bad, but they sure ended up with a great story to tell.

As my new fishing buddy and I finished our beers and stories he decided to head on his way to get some more fishing in. It wasn't long before the "poop" crew returned from the fuel dock. Now I got to hear another interesting "river" story. It seemed as they were approaching the fuel dock from the south the current was very strong and started to pull the boat off course. To correct the course of the boat they had to rev up the engines and get back on line, which caused a larger wake than normal.

Just south of the fuel dock is docked an older, very large, vessel that they passed close to during the course adjustment. After tying up at the fuel dock the "Admirals" took the dogs ashore for a break and our companion Captain noticed a man coming down to the fuel dock from the shore. The individual was pretty upset and stated that the Captain had caused a wake that had damaged his boat and one of his fenders. They went with him to his boat to see what the problem was and the fellow continued to question our friend's relationship to his mother with a lot of name calling. The Captain noted that the boat was very old and there was really no way to determine what damage was new or old on the side of the vessel as there was extensive wear and tear everywhere. The fender that was flat was so old and black with wear and mold it was hard to tell what had caused it to go flat and he really wasn't sure what to do at this point.

The fellow insisted that he was going to call the Sheriff and have the Captain arrested which caused the Captain to give it some thought. As this fellow kept his boat here all the time and probably knew everyone in a 50 mile radius and the Captain was from Minnesota, a northern state, it was probably in his best interest to just settle the matter immediately rather than discuss it further. He inquired what the fender was worth and the fellow stated he had just bought it for $100. The Captain paid him, got his crew back on board and headed out slowly telling himself to remember the river rule, always watch your wake.

ANXIETY FACTOR – HOW FAST CAN WE TRAVEL ON THE RIVERS?

Some boaters like to travel fast on the water and some like to travel slowly. For the "LOOPER" you will probably fall into the second group. Loopers just normally aren't in that much of a hurry.

Keep in mind that you want to try and stay away from having a set schedule you must abide by. You want to remain flexible in your time commitments especially on the rivers.

One rule you don't ever want to forget is that you are responsible for any damage that you may cause by the wake of your vessel and they take this very seriously along the rivers. The local river residents will call the police should you cause damage to their property whether intentional or not. If this should happen you will probably find a squad car waiting for you at the next lock.

Just take it slow and easy and always be aware of your surroundings and you will have no problems with this.

FEAR KNOT

When passing others vessels slow down and keep the wake to a minimum. They will appreciate it as would you. Try to contact the boat you are going to pass by radio to allow them to be prepared for the pass and agree on a passing side prior to the pass.

Should you find yourself in one of these wake damage situations just use that "common sense tool" and settle the matter as easy as possible before continuing on your way. You will thank yourself that you did.

After an interesting day for all I decided a treat would be in store for such a beautiful evening. I broke out the refreshments, fired up the grill and made dinner for both crews, some good old Milwaukee brats. It was a great evening and was enjoyed by everyone, including the two dogs who managed to get their share of the brats.

By the way, the dogs were Deedee, our 50 lb. Standard Poodle and our friend's dog Betty, a 160 lb. white Great Pyrenees. I guess I wasn't going to argue with them if they wanted brats.

While enjoying the quiet evening three other boats came into the channel to anchor near us. As I stated, this is a great area to spend the night and the more the merrier. As we were anchored so close together we all sat on the decks and had an evening of quiet conversation between all the boats.

We awoke to another beautiful day and all the boats in the Channel prepared to head out. The last two boats in were the first out and they headed on their way. The next boat was a 53 ft. Hatteras. They had put out both bow and stern anchors during the evening and decided to bring in the bow anchor first. As the bow anchor came up his boat started to drift into the opposite shore so he engaged an engine and sure enough, he now had a stern anchor line wrapped around a prop and shaft. The Captain stripped down to his cutoffs and into the water and mud he went, but his efforts were unsuccessful. It was decided that the only way to free the line was going to be to have the boat lifted out or a diver sent down. The really bad part was that they would have to cruise all the way up the Ohio River to Kentucky Lake to have the lift done or find a diver. Until then they would have to limp along on one engine. The good part is that the vessel has both the range and the power to make the journey so off we all went.

ANXIETY FACTOR – WILL WE HAVE TO ANCHOR OUR BOAT OUT?

I think that somewhere along The Great Loop you will find yourself anchoring out. Keep in mind that many Loopers anchor out every night and others prefer to stay at marinas. We enjoyed the marinas as we had a pet on board, but personal choice is all that matters.

FEAR KNOT

Anchoring is much less expensive and is great if you enjoy privacy and quiet. Either way you will enjoy those evenings on the water.

My only recommendation is that you be sure you have the proper ground tackle for different types of conditions. I would strongly recommend chain instead of line, if possible, due to some types of bottoms you may encounter. You should also consider extra ground tackle to allow you to run a bow and stern anchor or a Bimini (double) anchor should conditions make this necessary. Another thing to consider is an anchor release should you find yourself anchored in rocky or deadhead type bottoms where you may become snagged and have to get your anchor free.

GENE SCHNAGL

PHOTOS

Passing Mississippi barge traffic

Lunch on the go is on the bridge

FEAR KNOT

Caution, Mississippi River dredging

Mississippi River locking

Del Coronado tied up at Hoppie's Marina

Hoppie's Marina fuel dock

Kidd's Fuel Dock, Cape Girardeau, Mo.

Relaxing with fellow Loopers at Little Diversion River

FEAR KNOT

Kathy at the helm on the Ohio River

Passing heavy Ohio River barge traffic

Kathy making another Tow pass on the Ohio River

Fellow Looper up bound Ohio with a fouled prop

FEAR KNOT

The correct way to tie up to a floating bollard

GENE SCHNAGL

CHAPTER 5 – UP THE OHIO RIVER

The next run was going to be a super long one for us and fuel range became very important. There are only two ways to get to the Gulf of Mexico by boat on the rivers. You could continue south on the Mississippi river and head directly to New Orleans, but I would strongly not recommend this route. There are few fuel stops and no marinas on that stretch of the Mississippi. You also will encounter excessive tow traffic which can be very hazardous to recreational boaters.

The second route is the route we Loopers prefer. This requires going up the Ohio River to the Tennessee River and then heading south on the Tenn.-Tom, as the Tennessee Tombigbee Waterway is known, to Mobile, Alabama. Remember, you will need the fuel range to make it through the Kentucky Dam into the Tennessee River so allow yourself plenty of leeway.

We continued down the Mississippi to Cairo, IL and the turn up the Ohio River. It was a clear day and the junction at the Ohio was a sight to behold as there were tows with stacks of barges everywhere, in every direction. Due to conditions down in New Orleans after hurricane

Katrina, tow traffic was restricted and they were all backed up the rivers. When tow crews need to rest they don't have the ability to anchor out or find a nice slip at a marina like we do. Therefore it requires that a tow Captain perform a maneuver known as "banking". To accomplish this, he will direct his barges toward the bank of the river and push them right onto the bank. An engine is then kept running at low rpm to keep the boat and barges in position and the crew can get some rest.

In our case, tows and barges were sticking out of the shorelines like quills and were even on the shoals under the bridges. We decided to continue on, slowly weaving our way through the quills.

A couple of cautions I would offer you is, first, keep in constant radio communication with the tows as you work your way along. The tow captains will keep you informed as to how to progress safely. You also want to be sure to watch your charts for the channel and be sure to keep yourself centered, keep alert and be cautious.

ANXIETY FACTOR – IS IT DANGEROUS TO BE AROUND TOW BOATS AND BARGES ON THE RIVERS?

It isn't that you have to be afraid to be around tows and barges, it does, however, require that you be cautious. A tow with many barges takes an expert at the helm to control it and fortunately these Captains are experts. The problem lies in that many pleasure boaters don't understand that the tows cannot turn or stop on a dime. They are moving many thousands of tons and they cannot always see small vessels directly in front of them. Captains and crews are working for a living on the rivers and we are out there for pleasure. For the safety of all it is best that we rely on their experience and judgment in passing and meeting situations and follow their instructions.

I would recommend very strongly that you always keep in radio contact with Tow Captains and ask them how they would like you to pass them. They know what is best and appreciate the fact that you asked. They will also provide you with the safest instructions for maneuvering around them as they want to do everything they can to ensure your safety and theirs.

You will also want to watch yourself around tows as they have extremely large propellers and huge engines and their wakes can cause you to lose control of your boat in passing. Even though their wake may not appear that large they can create a lot of turbulence in the water just under the surface. Be prepared to correct if you feel yourself being pushed off course by this. Give yourself as much passing room as possible and be sure you stay in the river channel while doing so. Be prepared to turn into their wake as you pass to maintain control of your boat.

We made it through the traffic and were now headed northeast on the Ohio River. It was a clear sunshine day and Kathy took the helm for awhile to give me a break. Not only was it a

break for me but the Tow Captains seemed to enjoy looking at her as we passed much more than they enjoyed looking at me.

Sometime later I received a radio call from our companion boat. He stated that he was running low on fuel and didn't think he could make it to Kentucky Lake. After thinking about it I suggested two things. First, he should head into the landing at Paducah, Kentucky as we passed it. The landing is not for recreational boaters but running out of fuel would be an emergency. I advised that upon docking he should contact the Paducah Police by phone and advise them of his situation and request their advice and assistance. Secondly, I would be coming along side him and would pass over to him one of my extra fuel cans to use in case they ran out before reaching the landing.

We continued northeast and locked thru Lock #52 after which our companion boat turned off to Paducah for the night and we continued on. We later learned that the Paducah Police were very helpful. They took them to get fuel for their boat and showed them where to have a good dinner. The Police also advised them to just stay tied up for the evening and they would check on them occasionally to see if they needed anything. I guess as the old sayings goes, "it never hurts to ask" and "always ask for permission". You'll find a lot of "Good Neighbors" along the waterways.

ANXIETY FACTOR – WHAT IF WE ARE NOWHERE NEAR A PORT AND HAVE PROBLEMS?

What if you come around a turn in the river and the engine quits? Now what? For this reason I recommend, that as well as electronics and paper charts on your boat, that you also carry roadmaps for the areas you are traveling through. Nautical charts don't show you what is on the other side of the trees. With roadmaps you get an idea of what you are close to and many times assistance is just a few steps away from the shoreline.

Should problems occur that require help, try to get your vessel secured in a safe position, as far out of the navigational channel as possible, and then call 911 on your cell phone. 911 will connect you with the law enforcement response agency in your immediate area. Also put out an alert on your radio to let other boat traffic know where you are located to avoid any accidental collisions.

Always ensure that if someone is going to tow you, that you verify ahead of time that it is a tow and not salvage. Get a towing agreement in writing before that line is thrown to them. Give some thought to having towing insurance, as marine tows can be very expensive and towing coverage is just smart planning.

So, now we get to the fun part of the day. As our companion boat was so low on fuel and not wanting to leave them we kept our cruising speed to an absolute minimum. As a result, we were now running extremely late and night was upon us again. As I've said, if you can avoid it, never run after dark unless you have to. I've also said many times, to do as I say, not as I do. This brings us to our next incident on our journey.

It was way after dark as we approached the Kentucky Lock and Dam. This was going to be a 57 foot lift in the dark so we were taking it slow and easy. In communicating with the Lockmaster he advised me that I would have to go on hook in the holding pool for awhile. He had one down bound tow to get in and down before us. He also had an up bound tow banked on the starboard bank. His instructions were to anchor in the pool and after getting the down bound out he would move the up bound to the lock holding wall and have the Tow Captain hold position there. He would then take us through, before the up bound tow, just to get us out of the way. I advised we would be standing by and then heard the Lockmaster ask the up bound tow Captain if he copied. The up bound tow Captain stated that he copied just fine, but be sure to tell that boater to "stay the hell out of his way." Needless to say there was no further radio chatter after that last remark.

After a few hours of waiting the down bound was out and gone and the up bound was directed by the Lockmaster to proceed to the lower lock wall and hold. As the tow passed in front of us I decided to hoist anchor to be prepared for the lock. I then discovered that we had hooked a snag in the holding pond and I couldn't get the anchor up. With some tricky maneuvering I was finally able to free the anchor and it was then we noticed that the up bound tow had not held on the wall as directed by the Lockmaster but was going directly into the lock. I contacted the Lockmaster by cell phone and asked what was going on. The Lockmaster apologized and stated that this particular tow Captain was an individual they had numerous problems with and there was nothing he could do now but continue the locking procedure. I advised that I understood and proceeded to tie up on the lower lock wall for another few hour wait.

Sometime after 10:00pm we locked through and made it on to Kentucky Lake. Now all we had to do was cross the Lake, go through the Barkley Canal to Barkley Lake and we would be at Green Turtle Bay Marina for the night. So off we went across the lake.

As we left the lock we ran into solid fog bank where we couldn't see beyond the bow of the boat. Running on radar and chart plotter we worked our way across the lake to the opposite shore. All we had to do was find a channel just a little wider than our boat that we couldn't see in the dark. I was picking up what I hoped to be Channel markers on the radar and Kathy went out on the bow with a million candle power search light and I eased us toward shore. We located the canal and slipped thru to Barkley Lake. Now all we had to do is find the entry to Green Turtle Bay Marina.

I'm going to shorten this story by saying, good luck finding the channel to the marina in the dark. It seemed everywhere I was supposed to find the channel was a shoal or a shoreline. I finally decided to contact the Barkley Lock which I knew was just ahead of me in the fog. The Lockmaster was kind enough to direct me to go back to the buoy I had been at and then steer directly into the trees on shore on the port side. The channel runs right under the trees along the shore and I should be just fine. Everything worked great and we made it out of the fog and into the marina. During the daylight this would have been an easy entry but the darkness and fog had made it difficult.

FEAR KNOT

PHOTOS

Up bound port marker

Enjoying the sunshine on the Tennessee River

Tennessee River Lock open and waiting

Approaching a floating bollard wall inset

Green Turtle Bay breakfast with fellow Loopers

He broke down and we towed him in safely

FEAR KNOT

Entering Wheeler Lock

Joe Wheeler State Park

AGLCA Rendezvous

GENE SCHNAGL

Entering Wheeler Lock

Exiting Wilson Lock

Reaching the start of the Tennessee River

FEAR KNOT

Knoxville, Tennessee Marina

CHAPTER 6 – THE TENNESSEE RIVER

Day 16 we awoke with the sun shining, and the coffee smelling great. I checked in at the marina and they told us we could keep the slip we were at so we were all set.

After checking and finding that none of the other boats from Little Diversion had arrived we decided to head to the marina restaurant and have a great southern breakfast.

We later caught up on some laundry and boat cleaning which we really needed. I even took time to clean the fenders which really got filthy going through the locks.

ANXIETY FACTOR – DO WE NEED ANY SPECIAL EQUIPMENT TO GO THROUGH THE LOCKS?

Everyone gets concerned that their boat will get damaged in the locks. You really don't have to worry about it and you don't need any special equipment.

However, there are a couple of things I can suggest that might help you feel more comfortable. First, you might want to bring along gloves to protect the first mate or admiral's hands from the locks ropes, cables, etc. They can get pretty dirty or oily and gloves do help.

You also might want to consider oversized (locking) fenders. I usually use 10 inch fenders on our boat. Before we left I found two old 16 inch fenders someone had thrown out. I cleaned them as best I could and we made cloth covers for them that we could just throw away later. They worked great the entire voyage and really protected the bow and stern during locking. Many times when going up in a lock the fill water will try to twist your boat against the lock wall causing either the stern or bow to swing into the wall. The oversized fenders fore and aft prevented this from occurring many times for us.

Depending on the length of your boat you might also want to purchase inexpensive two way, voice activated communications to use while locking. This will save you and your crew from trying to yell directions to each other over the noise of the lock. Especially when he/she is all the way forward and you are all the way aft.

Later in the morning the other boats from Little Diversion began to arrive. The large Hatteras boat arrived on one engine. The next morning they hired a diver at the Marina and he found two five foot lengths of anchor rope wrapped around the prop and shaft. They were now returned to full service.

Later I received a cell phone call from the boat we had advised to go into Paducah Landing. They had refueled there but had run out of fuel again and were being towed into Green Turtle Bay. We planned to wait for their arrival.

We soon saw the trawler and 27 foot boat, which had left first from Little Diversion, coming into the marina. The interesting thing was that the trawler was towing the 27 foot boat. Guess who else had run out of fuel? Please note that the One Third Rule just keeps becoming more important every day.

Now that everyone had arrived safely Kathy made reservations at the Yacht Club for all of us for dinner and we had a great evening together. Everyone was back in great boating spirit.

ANXIETY FACTOR – DO WE HAVE TO BELONG TO A YACHT CLUB TO CRUISE ON THE LOOP?

Loopers are not required to belong to any organization. You may, however, want to consider joining your local Yacht Club before setting out as well as America's Great Loop Cruisers' Association.

Most Yacht Clubs that belong to the National Yachting Association have reciprocal agreements and are happy to have you come by their clubs and enjoy their facilities. This also allows you to meet the local members and gain a lot of local knowledge of the immediate area.

Upon arrival at a port check, see if there is a local club and give them a call. They usually have a great dining room and bar as well as knowledgeable and friendly members.

Day 18 - We have spent a couple of days exploring the surrounding country but now it is time to move on. It has been a wonderful couple of days with some fantastic local people we will not forget.

As we parted company with our Little Diversion friends we headed south on Barkley Lake and then back through the Barkley Canal and into Kentucky Lake. We turned south and were now headed up bound on the Tennessee River.

The Tennessee River is one of the most beautiful boating waters I have ever experienced. Every twist and turn brings more and new beautiful scenery to make you realize you really did make the right decision in cruising America's Great Loop.

It was such a great day and we made excellent time on the calm water. We decided to call it an early day and pulled into Cuba Landing Marina.

The Marina really isn't near anything but the owner told us to just take the van if we wanted to head to town. They treat you very well here and we really enjoyed our stay.

We decided to just have a quiet afternoon with Deedee so I opened a couple of cold beers and we went ashore and sat at a picnic table in the woods to just enjoy ourselves. Kathy and I watched the fishermen coming and going and the wildlife. Deedee proceeded to chew up sticks and may have chewed up enough to supply a Boy Scout camp with firewood for a week, but she was happy and that's what counts.

After a peaceful afternoon I made dinner on the boat and we turned in early. Tomorrow would be little longer run down to Pickwick State Park so we would head out a little early.

We will make the AGLCA Rendezvous at Joe Wheeler State Park just fine. We have made up our lost time and are back on a very relaxed timetable where we plan to stay.

Day 19 - We will finally hit what I call "The Big Locks." The Tennessee River has some of the largest locks in the United States so we are looking forward to a totally new experience in boating.

ANXIETY FACTOR – IS THE TRAFFIC ON THE TENNESSEE RIVER JUST LIKE THE MISSISSIPPI AND OHIO?

The Tennessee River is quite different than the other major rivers. Here you will not meet as much barge traffic, but you will experience a heavy increase in recreational traffic. Traveling on weekdays rather than weekends might be better if you can do it. On weekends there are numerous fishermen on the river and you must slow to NO WAKE constantly to avoid complaints about wakes. Be very cautious and alert on the river at all times as these fishing boats are hard to spot and are many *times tucked out of the way under tree branches, etc. My recommendation is to just take it slow and easy. The fishermen will thank you and you will appreciate the stress free cruise.*

Later in the afternoon we arrived at our only lock for the day. This is the 95 foot Pickwick Lock, which is a little intimidating as you slide into it. I'm still not sure what happened here, but for some reason the Lock Master made four other boats and us wait in an Auxiliary Lock for three and half hours while he kept letting down bound boats through one group after another. It was interesting, but I guess it's his lock, not mine. I do know there were some upset Captains, as I could hear the complaints over the roar of the lock purging the lock cells.

When we were finally allowed to lock through we arrived at Pickwick State Park Marina. The problem was, with the three and a half hour delay, we had to dock in the dark of night again. I guess you just have to expect these things and work with it. Now for a good night's sleep, if I can get Deedee to move over. Gee, that dog has long legs!

The next morning we were up and out on another beautiful day. The water is calm, but there was a little wind coming down the river. Actually the wind was blowing pretty good, but no problem at all.

ANXIETY FACTOR – IS WIND A BIG PROBLEM ON THE RIVERS LIKE ON THE GREAT LAKES?

On my home water of Lake Michigan just a breeze can mean you may have a rough ride ahead of you. We give the wind and the lake a lot of respect and wait for the right weather window before making a crossing.

Rivers are quite different. There were a couple of times in wide water areas with strong wind that we had 1-2 foot seas but that was about it. It is just not a problem.

One note though, is to remember that the channels can be narrow on a river and as the wind weaves down the river valley it can catch you off guard as you round a bend. Just be aware of your position on your charts and keep an eye on what is going on around you and you should avoid any problems.

Today is the day we will arrive at Joe Wheeler State Park and meet for some education and fun with the former and current Loopers. All we have to do is make it through two more of the "Big Locks." They will be Wilson and Wheeler which we are excited about going through.

ANXIETY FACTOR – HOW WILL WE KNOW WHERE TO TIE UP WHEN WE ENTER A LOCK?

Many times the Lock Master will tell you which side he wants you to tie up on so you won't have to guess.

When there are a number of boats entering together then the procedure may change. Boats will normally enter by "first come, first served" order. For this reason you may be prepared to tie up on the starboard side of the lock and suddenly find out that all the boats ahead of you wanted to do the same thing and there are no places left. This can cause you a problem as now your locking gear is on the wrong side of your boat.

Instead of finding yourself trying to hold position in the middle of the lock and having your deckhands running around trying to switch gear to the port side I have a recommendation for you.

Before entering a lock with multiple vessels Kathy had fenders and lines placed both port and starboard. That allowed us to be prepared for any tie up and we had no problems at all after we entered the lock and suddenly had to switch sides.

We made it through both locks with no problems or delays and just after Wheeler Lock we took our turn to port into First Creek and arrived at Joe Wheeler State Park. The park is a beautiful place with a very large lodge and marina and we were looking forward to a wonderful week.

I'm not going to go into a lot of detail about the next week except to say that if you are considering a cruise of The Loop then I would highly recommend that you make an AGLCA Rendezvous before and during your cruise. The amount of information you gain is extremely valuable as well as the many friends you will

make who may end up being on the Loop with you.

The Rendezvous is the time when you gain the information and answer the questions to assist in relieving any **ANXIETY FACTORS** that you may have.

After a wonderful week at Rogersville, Alabama we Loopers would normally start heading south down the Tenn.–Tom. In our case we did not do that for a couple of reasons.

The first is that there was a lot of Katrina damage down near Mobile, Alabama and they were still cleaning up. Quite a bit of southbound traffic was being restricted.

Secondly, and more importantly, is boat insurance. As our insurance would not cover us in the Gulf waters until a starting date of November 1, we decided we could dock the boat and fly home for awhile or we could just cruise the entire Tennessee River up and back, which we had never done. We decided on the latter and it turned out to be a great decision.

ANXIETY FACTOR – DO YOU NEED ANY SPECIAL INSURANCE FOR YOUR BOAT ON THE LOOP?

Never assume that your insurance policy covers you and your vessel at all times. Most boating policies are issued to cover you on specific waters at specific times of the year. This is normally as a result of such things as hurricanes, etc.

In our case we could not enter the gulf waters before November 1 and we had to be north of the Florida waters by July 1. Before or after those dates our insurance would not cover us should anything occur to us in the Gulf area.

Check with your provider in advance and be sure of your coverage.

Day 28 - We cleared Joe Wheeler and headed back out onto the Tennessee. The weather is good, the boat is running great, and we are feeling great. The Tennessee has got to be one of the most beautiful waterways I've ever seen.

I should point out something here to all of you, "get up and go", Great Lakes boaters. Normally on the Great Lakes we get up on plane to cross the big lakes. I think you will find that thought process changes very quickly when you hit the rivers.

Due to the wake problems, heavy traffic and narrow channels you will find that it is best to just take it slow and easy. I found that the best cruising speed for us was between 9 and 11 knots. It was easier on fuel, we enjoyed the scenery and it was much quieter traveling.

Besides, we just weren't in any hurry to get anywhere.

We spent the day cruising slowly until we reached a point about five miles south of Huntsville, Alabama. As we headed upriver I could see a fisherman standing in a bass boat near the starboard shore. He was waving his arms as if in distress so I slowed and pulled near him.

The fisherman informed us that he had been stranded there for a number of hours as his outboard engine would not start and now the battery was dead. A lot of boats had gone by but nobody would help him. I should point out that he was dressed in what some would call "gang" apparel, oversized baggy pants and a black sleeveless t-shirt with a skull on it. Pretty cool, huh?

Yes, we were cautious but I wasn't going to let anyone just sit there. Kathy threw him a tow line and I towed him the five miles to a marina where his car and trailer were.

After we made sure he got his boat out ok he came back to our boat at the dock to thank us. I asked if would like to join us for a cold drink and we had a soda together and talked. It was then we found out that he was a Sergeant in the US Army stationed at Redstone Arsenal. He lives off base with his wife and three kids.

I thanked him for his service to his country and wished him well from a fellow veteran. I also told him that he might want to consider different attire as a lot of boaters are old people like me and a little jumpy today. We laughed and he agreed he is going to start wearing "fishing" clothes from now on.

I guess it just goes to show that sometimes that "gut feeling" is right on and you have to go with it. This experience topped off a great day.

We decided to spend a day or so just touring around Huntsville so we pulled into Ditto Marina and got settled in. The next day we planned to unload the scooter and head to the Air and Space Museum in Huntsville.

ANXIETY FACTOR – HOW WILL WE GET TO STORES OR GO SIGHTSEEING IF WE ARE ON THE BOAT?

While you are on your cruise of The Loop you will have a number of alternative travel options while ashore. Normally you can rent a car while in port and the marinas can advise you of nearby dealers.

Many of the marinas have courtesy cars available at no charge to the transient boaters. You just refill the gas you use. If, however, there are a number of boaters seeking use of the car you may have to wait quite awhile or as we did many times, make new friends and travel in the courtesy car together. It can make for a fun time ashore.

In our case I also had constructed a small electric crane on the top of my aft deck. On my swim platform I had a Yamaha Zuma motor scooter. The reason for this particular one is that it does not require a motorcycle license, it has oversized off road tires for better balance on dirt roads and it would carry both Kathy and I at about 40-45 MPH. I would hook the crane lift straps and just lift it and set it on the dock and off we would go to shop, sightsee, or eat. It was fantastic.

You really won't have a problem getting around when you arrive in ports.

After a day spent seeing the sights in Huntsville we went out to dinner and then turned in early to head on up the river the following morning.

Day 30 – This morning cruising was slower than usual. We were hitting some patchy fog which required paying close attention to the instruments. We have to remember that we have radar, a chart plotter, and a depth sounder, etc. but the many fishing boats don't usually have anything but a sonar, and often no radio. You can see them, but they can't see you and they come at a good clip. Hitting the air horns usually works and slows them down in the fog, but be cautious.

In the late morning we arrived at the Guntersville Lock & Dam. With a tow and twelve barges ahead of us we had about a two hour wait so we dropped anchor in the holding area. And we did it again; we snagged the anchor and I had to work the boat around to bust it loose. There seems to be lots of snags in these holding areas and an anchor trip would be something useful to have.

After clearing the lock we headed up to Goose Pond Colony Marina, a beautiful resort to stay at. That evening we had dinner with a couple we had met at the AGLCA Rendezvous from New York State. We had a great evening and a great dinner.

ANXIETY FACTOR – CAN YOU CRUSIE THE GREAT LOOP IF YOU OR A CREW MEMBER HAS A PHYSICAL IMPAIRMENT?

I have met numerous individuals who tell me they would love to do this cruise but they have a serious physical impairment so they can't. I then like to tell them about some friends of ours who have completed The Loop on their boat. The couple from New York traveled with just the two of them. She was physically impaired and was limited to crutches or a motorized wheel chair.

He had a lift installed on board to lift the chair on and off their boat and it worked just great. When docking she would sit at the corner on the aft deck on the docking side of the vessel. They would call ahead for docking assistance and then as they neared she would throw the aft line to the dock handler. They rarely had any problem. All it seemed to take was a little thought adjustment, some team work and a great attitude.
Oh, and a big desire to see their dream fulfilled!

Day 31 – We headed out on another foggy morning just taking it slow. We had three boats traveling together now so we just cruised along nice and slow.

We only had one lock today and that was Nickajack Lock & Dam. We arrived at the Lock, but knew there were four other boats coming farther behind us. I advised the Lock Master about the other boats and told him we would be happy to wait for them and he said great and we just relaxed on the lock wall until they arrived.

I noticed something about the Tennessee today that I wanted to mention. In the Great Lakes we have a number of invasive species we are trying to contend with such as Zebra mussels, Asian Carp, etc. Here on the river they have encountered their own problem and that is Milfoil and Hydrilla. These weeds grow thick mats along the river and you do not want to get your props into the mats or you will be going nowhere fast. It requires you to keep watch as you travel so just be alert.

We parted company with the other boats and continued on to Hal's Bar Marina for the evening. The next morning we headed on to Chattanooga for some more sightseeing.

Day 32 – Another foggy morning, but it is patchy so no problem. I cannot begin to tell you how stunning the scenery is cruising thru these mountain valleys. It gets difficult to keep your eye on where you are going as there is so much beauty around you.

We made it to Chattanooga just fine, but there was a mess up at the Marina regarding our reservation so we continued on to another small marina. Our stay wasn't the best because they had very poor docks and the power kept going out. I have to admit though, that the food at their small country restaurant was home cooking and we did have a very good meal that evening.

Day 33 – We pushed on the next morning and locked through Watt's Bar Lock and up Watt's Bar Lake toward the marina we planned on spending the evening at. Kathy tried to call them on the cell but kept getting a disconnected number message. Upon arrival we found out why, the marina wasn't in existence any longer even though it was still listed in the Waterway Guide.

No problem, we just headed on to the next one. This turned out to be a blessing as we decided to stay at Euchee Marina. This is a quaint little marina tucked into a beautiful small bay with a

fantastic restaurant and bar. Not in the Waterway Guides, it was truly a hidden treasure. We will be back.

It was so nice at Euchee we decided to stay for a couple of days. So I unloaded the motor scooter and we set out exploring. We headed to the nearby community of Spring City, Tennessee and stocked up on supplies. It was just great riding the scooter along the small back country roads.

We then headed to Ten Mile, Tennessee and did the laundry. I think it's called Ten Mile because it is ten miles from anywhere and everywhere. While waiting for the wash Kathy explored a nearby thrift shop. I walked to a sport shop across the road where some of the local "good ole' boys" were sitting out on the porch. I got a cup of coffee with them and learned a lot about the local fishing and hunting. All I can say is, these are great folks down here in Tennessee, very friendly and open. Just be careful where you walk in your bare feet. These guys chew a lot of tobacco and can spit a long way. I turned down the chew but they still let me sit in the chewing area with them. I love this country!

Day 34 – We only have about 100 miles left until we reach the start of the Tennessee River. We decided to make this a short day so we locked through the Fort Loudoun Lock and turned into the Fort Loudoun Marina. Fort Loudoun was another very scenic area so we unloaded the scooter and decided to spend an extra day exploring.

That evening we met two couples from Minnesota and decided we would all have dinner at the marina restaurant. We experienced another wonderful evening with great boating people.

The next day we took the scooter into Lenoir City, Tennessee and checked out the Mega Wal-Mart. Kathy got her nails done and I got a haircut. We did some shopping, grabbed some lunch and then headed on back to the marina.

ANXIETY FACTOR – HOW WILL I FIND PLACES TO GET MY HAIR CUT, NAILS DONE, ETC.?

Like most gals, Kathy can be very picky about where she has her hair cut or her nails done. On the cruise we didn't find this to be a problem. She always seemed to find a local gal who would suggest someone close by that we could go to and it always seemed to work.

As for my haircuts, I'm really am not too picky as, at my age, after all, I only have a few hairs left to worry about. A good local barber is not hard to find anywhere along The Great Loop.

We did find that the large stores such as Wal-Mart were the best one-stop shopping providers for us and seemed to be located at almost every large port.

Tomorrow we head out to Knoxville, Tennessee which will be the turnaround point for us on the Tennessee River.

Day 36 – after a beautiful sunny day on the water we arrived in Knoxville, Tennessee, where we had made a reservation at the Volunteer Marina. You should know that the University of Tennessee is just a few blocks from the marina and they are the UT Volunteers so everything is named Volunteer in Knoxville.

It was a little tricky getting into the slip on the river but we handled it just fine. This river boating seems to get easier and easier with every day on the water.

ANXIETY FACTOR – ARE THERE ANY PROBLEMS WITH DOCKING ON THE RIVERS?

As mentioned earlier in the book, the current is the one of the factors that can give you a problem on the rivers. You always want to dock into the current.

The Volunteer Marina entry presented a different type of current problem as the slips are covered and are perpendicular to the river. That means that as you make your slip entry the current is pushing against the side of your vessel which can create a problem.

The solution is to come toward the slip upriver from the slip entry. Ease the bow up to the end of the slip docks and let the current carry you down river. As your bow comes to the slip opening slide in easy and you should have no problem.

Should you miss the entry just back out and start over. Don't be embarrassed, everyone has missed at one time or another, whether they admit it or not.

Knoxville is a fun city to visit as they have a free trolley system that takes you around town. They also have a number of great restaurants along the river front. We had lunch at the Patrick O'Sullivan Saloon and Cathouse. The food was great. It was interesting though, in the sense, that upstairs above the bar they had all these small rooms. I just couldn't figure out why they would want to keep cats in little rooms like that. Oh well, I'm from up north, what do I know?

After lunch we caught the trolley again to Market Square where Kathy hit the shops. I sat in the garden area with a cup of coffee and kept my eyes open for any of those cats from the Saloon. I guess they were sleeping because I didn't see any.

FEAR KNOT

We later went back to the boat and sat on the aft deck with a drink before dinner and watched the UT rowing teams running sprints behind our boat on the river. Life is good!

Day 38 – We headed out to cover the last four miles of the 400 miles of the Tennessee River. The current was very strong this morning and lots of tree limbs in the water. There were some storms northeast of us and I think we just found out they were bad. We'll just take is slow and easy.

In a short time we made it to the top of the river where the Holston and the French Broad rivers come together to form the Tennessee River. We took our photos and turned to start our long, but enjoyable, journey back. We are really glad that we decided to do this side trip as it was well worth it, but now it is time to head back down the river and get back on The Great Loop course again

GENE SCHNAGL

CHAPTER 7 – THE TENNESSEE RETURN

Day 39 – We have started our return down the Tennessee River. I am not going to write about a lot of the return as it pretty much the same as when we headed up.

We had no difficult locking incidents, although we did have a little rough weather off and on for part of the way. All and all it was great until we arrived at Alred Marina which is near Huntsville, Alabama.

Our reason for staying here is that I had to be near a major airport so Kathy could fly to Las Vegas. We had received a cell call while on the river advising that one of Kathy's old friends was close to passing from a terminal disease. The marina loaned me the courtesy van and I drove her to the airport in Huntsville for a flight out. She planned to be in Las Vegas about a week and that would give me time to get caught up on chores on the boat. This is one of those unplanned incidents that can just happen when you are on an extended journey.

ANXIETY FACTOR – WHAT IF WE HAVE AN EMERGENCY AT HOME WHILE WE ARE ON THE WATER?

With the numerous marinas along The Great Loop route emergency trips home are not usually any problem to respond to. You will normally find a major airport in a nearby city or a car rental. The marinas are very good at taking care of your boat while you are gone and you will be surprised just how helpful the marina operators are. They are, as a group, a wonderful bunch of individuals who are more than happy to assist their customers.

With Kathy gone I set about catching up on chores. As a result another unplanned incident occurred. I was on the forward deck cleaning fenders, which badly needed cleaning after all the locks. I was attempting to untangle the wash hose and backed up a step. As I did so my right foot went down in the chain cut for the anchor and I did it! I broke my right big toe. It was now at a right angle to the rest of my toes.

I won't say it hurt, but "Big Boys" do cry. I limped to the aft deck and sat trying to decide if I should head to a hospital or just bend it back. I decided to just bend it back and tape it to the rest of my toes. I got it done all right but I can't say it was the best idea I ever had.

It still has a pretty good bend in it but I tell my grandchildren it's just Grandpa's "Monkey Toe" and I can climb trees with it and peel bananas just like monkeys do. What the heck, it works for me!

Kathy made it back ok and had a comforting trip to see her friend. We are just happy that she was able to make it in time. It was one of those important moments that really count in life.

Day 52 –The next day we headed south to Decatur, Alabama. I guess the marina we stayed at is what you would term "rustic". The shore water didn't work, the cable TV didn't work, the power sometimes worked and the finger docks are only 25 feet in length while my boat is 42 feet in length. Other than that it was great.

The marina restaurant was also pretty "rustic". It was packed with people, but you couldn't tell as much as you tried to see through the cloud of smoke. I did notice that there were a lot of pretty gals in the place and they all tended to be built like Dolly Parton. I wasn't sure why but then I figured it must be because they have a longer growing season in the south compared to us up north. I mentioned this to Kathy and my arm still hurts. Why don't Admirals come with a sense of humor?

They did have an awesome catfish sandwich so it was worth the sore arm. Also, just as we were going to leave four big guys with full beards and long hair came in with guitars and the largest speakers I have ever seen. I think their names were Bubba, Bubba, Bubba and Little Bubba. They started playing great, but very loud, country music. We decided to head to bed early even though the music was actually very good.

I can only say it was an interesting evening as we were rocked gently to sleep on our boat to the soothing sounds of the Bubba Boys, the rap of air brakes on 18 wheelers coming down the mountain road beside the river and the mellow tones of the train whistle from the local train crossing about 100 yards away. I guess not every stop is perfect but some are just better than others. Its memories like this that make you glad you decided to make this trip. What a great nation we live in with it's never ending variety.

Day 53 – Our first stop this morning was Wheeler Lock & Dam. The lock master let us right in and we got tied up easily. A couple of fancy bass boats came in at a good clip with guys on board dressed like they were pro fishermen or something. I told Kathy that a lot of these guys down south think that if they get a fancy bass boat with a big engine and dress like pros they will catch more fish. Yea, right!

We next headed into super big Wilson lock and got tied up easy again. Then a whole pile of fancy bass boats came roaring into the lock. It was then I noticed that there was a helicopter hovering over us with a cameraman in it and I realized that the guys actually were pro bass fisherman and that there was a cameraman in each boat with the fisherman.

The chopper was filming above us and we were on national TV that evening.

It seems that we had got caught up in a major bass fishing competition and the purse was three million dollars. I would have got my fishing rod out if I had known that earlier.

We cleared the lock after the bass boats left and later pulled into the Mystic River Marina for the night. Guess where the fishing tournament was based out of? It made for an exciting evening and a lot of fun. I did have to make Kathy promise not to tell any of the pros about my crack regarding southern bass boats. If she had told them, I think I would have found out what it feels like to be bass bait!

ANXIETY FACTOR – *IF WE HAVE A PET ON BOARD WILL WE BE ABLE TO FIND CARE FOR THEM ALONG THE WAY?*

Most of the marinas will be near a town where you will be able to find a vet or a groomer, if needed. We never had a problem finding needed services along THE LOOP. Just be sure all pet health records are up to date before you depart and bring copies along to verify them.

Day 55 – Today we arrived at Grand Resort Marina at the very top of the Tenn.-Tom. (Tennessee Tombigbee Waterway). We are ready to head south to the Gulf.

Grand Resort is a great location to stop at with wonderful services. We even got to take a courtesy vehicle and head to Shiloh Battlefield for some great American history lessons.

Being at Grand Resort Marina is unique as while you are sitting on your boat you are actually in the state of Mississippi. As you look to the east across the channel you are looking at Alabama and if you look north you are looking into Tennessee. It's a great place to take a break and get rested up.

FEAR KNOT

PHOTOS

Grand Resort at the top of the Tenn.-Tom.

Watch out for car ferries

Clean cut Tenn.-Tom. banks

The Rooster Bridge site on the Tenn.-Tom.

Following the swamp stakes to Aberdeen Marina

Following the stakes carefully

FEAR KNOT

Sunset at Midway Marina on the Tenn.-Tom.

Rafted up at Bobbie's Fish Camp

Dinner arriving at Bobbie's Fish Camp

GENE SCHNAGL

CHAPTER 8 – THE TENNESSEE TOMBIGBEE WATERWAY

Day 57 – We are finally headed toward the Gulf of Mexico and we are going to see if we can make it to Tarpon Springs, Florida for Thanksgiving with Kathy's parents.

Traveling the Tenn.-Tom. is beautiful but caution is needed. There are many twists and turns and the channels get narrow and shallow at times. There also seems to be a lot of barge and tow traffic around every turn so passing becomes a concern. Taking it slow and easy is the rule of the day and will get you through without incident.

ANXIETY FACTOR – I'VE HEARD STORIES OF BOATERS GETTING SHOT AT DOWN SOUTH, ARE THEY TRUE?

I've heard the same stories and I honestly can't tell you if they are true or not. What I can tell you is that if you watch your wake carefully you shouldn't have any problems.

Property owners and local residents can get a little upset with all the boater traffic and with some of the inconsiderate boaters I have seen they probably have good cause. Being respectful of their property and a courteous boater seems to eliminate any reason for concern.

We only had one incident where someone yelled at us but that was one I couldn't do much about. We were only going about *nine knots but as I came around a bend in the river someone started yelling and swearing at us. I couldn't see a soul but then just happened to notice out of the corner of my eye two fishermen in a camouflaged duck boat, with a camouflaged painted outboard, wearing camouflaged clothing, with camouflaged hats anchored along the shore bank under a large tree branch which extended down to the water. They were upset because I didn't slow for them. I really didn't think there was anything I wanted to say that would help the matter so I just waved with a friendly smile, mouthed "sorry" and we continued on. I found it interesting that they required concealment to fish. I honestly wasn't aware of the fact that concealment was a fishing necessity. That probably explains why I never catch that many fish, I'm hard to conceal.*

Just be careful, apologetic, slow and alert and there shouldn't be any cause for worry.

Day 58 – We locked through three locks today and cruising is going great. Lots of morning fog, but it burns off pretty fast and then we move out. Seems to be a lot of debris in the water, tree branches, etc. from some of the storms we've had in the area. Kathy is spotting them as lookout and we are avoiding the big stuff.

We decide to stay at Aberdeen Marina tonight, which is a pretty little marina back off the Tenn.-Tom. You have to weave through a swamp to get there, but it is really a neat trip.

We ran into two gals doing The Loop together on a 24 foot cruiser with their cats and dog, Two sweet school teachers on an adventure.

FEAR KNOT

They told us they had the courtesy car and asked us to join them in driving into the local town for dinner.

I thought this would be the perfect time to have Kathy get away from the testosterone for a little while and suggested that the three of them go, as I had some chart work I wanted to get done and Deedee and I could make some dinner for ourselves. Off the gals went with no argument.

When Kathy returned later that evening she told me it had been a great idea. They talked about gal things and about what books to read and just had a great evening. Wow, I guess even I have a good idea once in a while!

Day 59 – Only two locks today and then we'll spend the evening at Marina Cove. On this stretch, this is the only Marina to stay at or you have to anchor out. It was a little shallow for us, but I made it into the fuel dock to refuel and then got tied up.

Kathy took Deedee ashore to do her job and then play some "chase the ball" for awhile. A while later she returned with a very muddy dog. It seems that the ball rolled down a bank and right out on top of the Hydrila which was taking over the shoreline. Deedee thought it was just grass, kept running to get the ball and sank. She got the ball, but in swimming back, got covered in mud. It looks like bath time for mom and dog tonight.

Day 60 – Today is our wedding anniversary, 11/11/05, so I have a choice. Either we anchor out tonight or I make a 95 mile run and get to Demopolis, AL. and a marina to take her out for dinner. I decided to make the run for dinner so I could guarantee another anniversary after this one.

We made it to Demopolis Marina without a problem, but found out the marina was totally packed. Many of the boats are heading south now after waiting out all the hurricane damage. After talking with the dock master and refueling, she told us to just stay on the fuel dock for the night and to have a good time.
We got Deedee settled in, got cleaned up, and headed out for a night on the town. It wasn't exactly a town; there was only one bar/restaurant in the area. It was packed to the ceiling and the bluegrass music was loud and good, and every guy in the bar had a beard, including me, so it must have been a good place.

I was going to order lobster and wine for two but we settled for a catfish sandwich and a Mo' burger with fries. That and two beers made for a fantastic anniversary dinner. We then called it a pleasant and early evening.

Day 61 – We started the day with another morning of heavy fog. I decided to skip the race to the lock with all the other boats and called the lockmaster who gave me a horn toot after the fog lifted. We then headed into the lock and were on our way to the famous/infamous Bobbie's Fish Camp, our last stop before Mobile, Alabama and the Gulf.

ANXIETY FACTOR – DO WE HAVE TO ALWAYS START OUT EARLY TO GET THROUGH THE LOCKS?

Many boaters feel the need to head out before the sun rises to get a full day of boating in. They also want to be the first in the locks so they don't have to wait for another lock opening.

My personal opinion is that this is not always the smartest move to take. As I've stated, the rivers and especially the Tenn.-Tom. experience a heavy amount of early morning fog. What many recreational boaters don't know is that the Tow Captains don't like to run in the fog. For this reason they will pull their tow and barges into a lock in the late afternoon and get tied up. They will then spend the night in the lock to allow the crew to get some sleep. In the morning the Lock Master will not open the lock until the fog has lifted and the tow is ready to head out.

I found that many times the boats in the marinas would race each other out in the fog to get into the lock and find the lock not open. They would then circle around in the fog bumping into things and each other during their wait, which can prove to be a little risky.

Rather than leave my slip early I would call the lock master by phone and just ask him when he planned to open. A number of times I was informed they had a "sleeper in the cell". I would then ask if he could just give me a whistle when he planned to get ready to open and I would pull lines and head over. They were always happy to do so and usually we were the first in the lock.

Don't be in a hurry and get yourself into danger when you don't have to.

Day 61 – We arrived at Bobbie's Fish Camp. We fueled up first and then got tied up to Bobbie's dock. They only have one long 150 foot dock here so as the boats arrive they get rafted with the last boat. They can be, maybe three boats out in the channel. Being the outside boat can get a little nerve racking as the Tows and barges keep traveling by all night long and the channel gets narrow here. Try to arrive at Bobbie's in the mid to late afternoon, but no later.

We rafted another boat to us later in the afternoon and the dock filled up fast. That evening we had a fresh catfish dinner at Bobbie's and a fun filled evening. Another early to bed evening and we were ready to head to Mobile.

ANXIETY FACTOR – DOES THE WATERWAY CHANGE BELOW BOBBIE'S FISH CAMP?

Below Bobbie's Fish Camp you will hit your last lock on the Waterway from the Tennessee River to the Gulf of Mexico. It will be the Coffeeville Lock and Dam.

You will need to remember that from this point on you will now be in tidal waters. You must be aware of this as the tides will now affect your slip tie ups, anchorages and drafts throughout the day with the tidal changes.

For Inland Boaters this will be a big change and constant awareness is a necessity until you get used to the tidal changes.

Day 62 – Instead of anchoring out for the night we made a 140 mile run straight to Mobile Bay today. We made our last lock on the Tenn.-Tom. and Kathy is happy to take a breather from all the locking for awhile.

This stretch of the Waterway gets very twisty so you may find the going a little tense. The boat traffic seemed to be getting heavier as well as the barge traffic, so we just stayed alert and did not encounter any problems.

Later in the day we could see the high Interstate 65 Bridge ahead and the Mobile, Alabama ship yards; we had arrived at Mobile Bay. After so long on the rivers it seems odd to see the waters of the Bay open up before us. It was going to be a big change but one we had been looking forward to.

Our choice had been to stay at East Shore Marine in Fairhope, Alabama on the east side of the Bay. We followed the channel markers on the west shore line until the mid bay crossing and then wove our way across the Bay to Fairhope on the east shore. We had completed the Tennessee Tombigbee Waterway and were beginning a new phase of America's Great Loop.

ANXIETY FACTOR – WHERE SHOULD WE STAY IN MOBILE BAY AND CAN WE CROSS THE BAY ANYWHERE WE WANT?

Mobile Bay offers numerous opportunities for laying up a day or two. Marinas and anchorages are many and your Waterway Guides will provide you with the information you need.

Many sail boaters, who must step their masts up north to head down the rivers, have the masts shipped by truck to a Mobile marina pick them up when they arrive here.

Cruising Mobile Bay however, requires you watch your charts very closely. The Bay is extremely shallow and the channels must be followed at all times. Never just wander about!

The crossing channels on the Bay are not straight courses and will require that you go from marker to marker, changing course along the way. Keep a watchful eye on your charts and remember your tide tables for the Bay; you are in tidal waters now.

FEAR KNOT

PHOTOS

Bottom of the Tenn.-Tom., Mobile Bay

On the bottom when the tide went out on Mobile Bay

GENE SCHNAGL

Eastport Marina, Fairhope, Alabama

Intercoastal from Mobile to Pensacola

Tied up at Destin, Florida Marina

Dinner guests on board at Apalachicola

CHAPTER 9 – THE INTERCOSTAL WATERWAY

Day 63 – We are enjoying Fairhope, Alabama a lot. Kathy was able to get her nails done again and with no locks for quite awhile she is really happy. I'm getting things caught up on the boat and with the courtesy car we have met a number of new friends and are doing a lot of exploring.

The damage from Hurricane Katrina is still quite obvious and work is still being done to clean up the area. Many of the boats at the marina were destroyed and there were thirty boats from across Mobile Bay that were blown all the way to Fairhope Marina and piled up. Now you know the reason why the insurance companies do not cover you before November 1st and want you back out of Florida waters by July. Avoiding the Hurricane Season is a must for boaters.

Day 66 – After waiting out some storms for a few days we decided it was time to push on. We finally awoke this morning to no wind and nice sunny weather. Kathy made the comment that after all the high winds she slept great last night, as the boat didn't rock at all.

After getting my coffee I went up on deck and told Kathy to come up and I would show her why the boat didn't rock. It seemed that the strong winds during the night and an overly strong tide had pushed all the water out of Mobile Bay. Our boat, which was normally in eight feet of water, was now setting on the bottom with no water.

We had to wait for the tide to come back in and then decided to head out. As we cleared the slip and entered the channel I heard a loud noise and felt heavy vibration on the port shaft. I shut down the engine and we limped into the fuel dock. We were going to be spending another night so we could lift the boat out in the morning and find out what damage was done to the port shaft or prop and figure out what I had hit.

The following morning we had the boat lifted and found a large bimini top wrapped around both our props. It looks like Katrina got us after all. There is still a lot of debris left from the hurricane that you have to watch out for and the water is very shallow in Mobile Bay. We'll be keeping very alert from now on. After paying our bill we were on our way to finally take on the ICW (Intercoastal Waterway).

FEAR KNOT

ANXIETY FACTOR – WHAT DO WE DO IF WE PICK UP DEBRIS OR THINGS LIKE CRAB POTS?

I can feel safe in telling you that somewhere while on America's Great Loop you will probably find that you will have something tangled around your propeller. I have yet to meet a Looper who hasn't experienced these problems at least once during their adventure.

How often this happens and how big of a problem you incur will depend on you so let's discuss them one at a time.

Tangling a prop can be caused by a number of things, weeds, debris or most commonly a crab pot. On the inland rivers it would probably be Hydrilla. Weeds like this can foul props quickly. The other issue might be fish nets.

With weeds you will need to reverse props and try to back out the same way you came in. By forward and reversing you may be able to clear your props.

Fish nets are going to require that you either hire a diver to go under to clear the prop and shaft or if you are qualified and have the proper equipment you can do this yourself. Either way, they must be cleared before you continue, so be prepared.

In coastal waters and areas like Chesapeake Bay you will find the infamous crab pots. Crab pots are not allowed to be set in navigable channels, however they can usually be found there. I have been told that this is caused by the tides and things like wind, but I'm not so sure. Whatever the cause, you will need to dive to clear them from your props and shafts. Should you experience this, shut that engine down and get yourself to a place of safety. After anchoring or tying up at a slip you can address the problem.

On the Great Lakes you will encounter commercial fish nets. The nets are placed perpendicular to the shoreline and the ends of the nets will be marked by floating "Fish Stakes". This is *usually a floating marker brightly colored with a vertical height of about 4 -5 ft.*

The nets extend down to bottom depth from the stakes so you can cruise right over the net. Should you encounter a fish stake just stay well clear of the stake and continue on your way and you should have no problem, however, should you tangle a fish net you will have to clear the prop before continuing.

Day 67 – We are on our way again and running a zigzag course down Mobile Bay to keep clear of the shoals. Watching your charts carefully on Mobile Bay is a must.

Lucky for us that I was cruising slowly because as we approached Mile Marker 120, which is the turn point for the ICW, I found that the tide had carried us a little off course and I slid onto a sand shoal. We had finally gone aground.

After my heart attack passed, I backed off and corrected course and we continued up the ICW with no further problems. Another beautiful cruising day was headed our way.

ANXIETY FACTOR – WHAT HAPPENS IF WE GO AGROUND?

The one thing you can be sure of on America's Great Loop is that you will most likely go aground at least once. With the thousands of miles you will be cruising the law of averages is just against you. This is not an issue that will cause you great problems if you handle it properly.

As I've already discussed, you should be going slow most of your journey and you should be watching your charts carefully. That being said, buoys get moved, shoals change and you are going to find one.

If you find yourself going aground, put your engines in neutral immediately. Determine if your props are still free and if it is just the bow aground. If so, you will probably be able to back your vessel off the shoal and continue on your way. This works well in sandy or muddy bottoms, but when in Canada be very careful as the bottoms and shoals are rock and heavy damage to the hull could be possible. In this case, after backing off the shoal, be sure to check below for leaks before continuing on your way.

If you find yourself severely grounded you may try carrying an anchor out by dinghy and winching off or you may have to call for a tow which can be expensive. Think your way through your situation and determine just how bad you are stuck and what you are stuck on and then take action.

After grounding if you engage the engines and feel heavy vibration you may have damaged a shaft or a prop and this will require the earliest possible repair before further cruising. Consult your Waterway Guides for the nearest available full service center.

After a short run up the ICW we entered Pensacola Bay which is a fairly large open body of water about 13 miles long and 2 ½ miles wide. As we left the ICW we found the winds were very high and we now had 4-5 ft. seas in the Bay. As we had a reservation at the Palafox Marina in Pensacola it was going to be a long, rough ride. After an interesting 13 mile

ride up the Bay we made it safely to the marina and spent a quiet, but windy, evening in Pensacola.

Day 68 – The day was calm and clear and we left Pensacola, down the Bay and back into the ICW. We cruised our way up to an area called The Narrows with no problems. The Narrows consists of a lot of shoals and you have to be alert, but the water was clear and the shoals easy to spot.

We decided to cut the day a little short and obtained a slip at Harborwalk Marina in Destin, Florida. This was an excellent stop as the fishing charters are all here and we walked the Charter Dock during the late afternoon. There is lots of fresh fish coming in and on display on the docks. I think Deedee thought she had died and gone to heaven. I guess we'll have fresh fish for dinner this evening and enjoy the sunset. Tomorrow we will be heading to Panama City, Florida.

Day 69 – It was a long run today to Panama City and our luck turned a little for the worse, weather wise. The winds have picked up again and the rain came in. We had following seas, which helped, but the waves are about four feet on the many wide bays we have to cross so the going is a little choppy. With all the heavy rain, visibility is getting limited so Kathy is aiding me with the navigation, which is another great help. I'm glad I have a mate who really knows what she is doing.

We made it into the marina in Panama City and with the weather getting worse by the minute I fueled up first. Getting into our slip in the high winds was a little tricky, but Kathy and I are working like a true team now and it went pretty easy. I'm not so sure that we are going to make it to Tarpon Springs, Florida in time for Thanksgiving. We will surely need a weather window for a Gulf crossing and things aren't looking too promising. I guess we'll know in another day or two.

Day 70 – We woke to high winds again this morning, but the rain has died down. I had hoped to make a sixty mile run today but the weather may shorten that.

As the day progressed the winds kept increasing and holding position in the ICW Channels was getting a little tricky. We didn't have a lot of depth outside the channels so it was a much focused day at the helm. When we hit the bays the waves were in the three to four foot range and it was rough, but we continued on our way.

Two other boats had left Panama City with us but one had decided to turn back so we continued on our way with just the two of us. Later in the morning we had made it across the bays and into the sheltered canals, so the going got easier.

It was nice to know that we were being watched over, as we received a cell call from the marina we had left checking on our condition. The winds were so bad at Panama City that they had eight to ten foot waves breaking over the marina seawall. We thanked them for their concern and advised that the one boat had turned back. We were informed that they had made it safely so we continued on. If we hadn't left when we did we would have been stuck there for a few days at least. Weather windows are everything to boaters and ours was closing down fast.

In the afternoon we finally made it to Scipio Marina in Apalachicola, Fl., and our destination for today. We tied up in 20 knot winds and called it a day. We would have liked try to continue on to Carrabelle, Florida before crossing, but that was not to be. With the rough weather, boats were waiting and the marinas

FEAR KNOT

filling up so we could go no further. Now we wait for some calm seas.

CHAPTER 10 – CROSSING THE GULF OF MEXICO

Day 71 – We ran into some old friends from Bobbie's Fish Camp and decided that our four boats will try to make a night crossing in a day or so if we get the weather we need. Until then we will get ready and just relax. I purchased four extra six gallon fuel cans to take some reserve with us just in case.

ANXIETY FACTOR – WHEN AND WHERE SHOULD WE CROSS THE GULF?
The two main ports for the Gulf crossing on the Great Loop are Apalachicola and Carrabelle, Florida. They are the closest ports to the "Panhandle." From there you will have a couple of options, either follow the coast around toward Crystal River and down the Florida coast or run straight down the Gulf offshore to your next port such as Tarpon Springs or Clearwater, Florida.

Most boaters will want to run at night after the winds have died down and will arrive at their destinations around daybreak. They will also run in a group of boats for safety. Finding others to cross with is never a problem from either of the start ports.

The best thing to do is not be in a hurry and wait for your weather window. The marinas will keep you informed of when a good start time is and which the best route is for you.

Day 72 – As always the plans have changed again. We were advised that there would be a weather window during the day but it would

close again that night and it may be many days before another opportunity. The group decided we would make the go this morning and make a day crossing. We'll have to see how things go.

As we had committed not to leave a boat alone we told two of the boats to go ahead and we would wait for the last boat as they seemed to be a little slow in getting started. The first two boats headed out about daybreak and we waited. Around 9:50am the last members of our group finally came over and said they had changed their minds last night, slept in, and forgot to tell anyone about their change of plans.

Needless to say, we were somewhat upset, and for this reason, I proceeded to make a poor decision. Kathy and I headed out late on our own and had a lot of time to make up, but I wanted to be in Tarpon Springs for Thanksgiving, as I had promised Kathy and her parents I would be. Remember, the number one rule in cruising, never ever commit yourself to a schedule! I was now breaking that rule.

After clearing Government Gap, we changed course and were now headed toward Crystal River, Florida. We only had about 139 miles to go to hit our marker and then change course again down the Florida coast to Tarpon Springs.

As expected the winds picked up during the day but the seas were only 2-3 feet with about four foot swells so it was just fine. The wind was also out of the north and was supposed to stay that way so we would have following seas into the evening and that would be perfect even if the winds kept picking up.

Toward late afternoon we hit our marker off of Crystal River, right on the button and I changed course south. We were on the last leg to Tarpon Springs. Now came the time that I would have to conserve fuel. We had been running on plane to make up for lost time so my fuel consumption was much higher. I knew I was going to have to add fuel from the spare cans and it was just a matter of when. I would just have to keep my eye on the gauges and hope the seas calmed down a little.

As the sun started to set our luck started to set with it. I had slowed to about 9-11 knots to conserve on fuel. Even though the weather report had stated that the winds would continue out of the north during the evening I noticed we were getting a wind shift. The wind was now out of the west and building and the waves went up to around 5-6 feet. We were now taking the seas on the starboard beam and it was going to be a long dark night.

After reviewing our options I decided to continue on. If we tucked in somewhere we could be stuck there for up to a week and I was just, I guess, too stubborn to stop, which in hindsight was a mistake. We would just see how the night went. I was still comfortable with the weather and seas, at least for now.

ANXIETY FACTOR – WHAT IF WE ARE ON THE GULF AND A STORM COMES UP, HOW WILL PEOPLE KNOW WHERE WE ARE?

This question brings up one of the rules the Coast Guard is always cautioning us about, file a Float Plan before you clear the harbor. Filing a Float Plan doesn't have to mean a lot of paperwork. Just letting someone know the route you plan on taking that day and your expected time of arrival at your destination can be a life saver. If you should experience a change in weather while at sea contact the Coast Guard and let them be aware of your situation and they will monitor you for safety purposes. They are really very good at their job if you just follow their instructions.

At around 7:00pm we received a radio call from the U.S. Coast Guard, St. Petersburg, Florida. They requested I switch to 22 Alpha and advised me that they had received a call of concern for our safety from a party named Joan in Tarpon Springs, Florida.

FEAR KNOT

To shorten this story let me just say that when you tell your mother-in-law that you will call her after you make the turn at Crystal River, Florida, just make sure that you do call and also that you can make the call from out at sea. I had told her that I would, but then found we were too far off the Florida Coast for a cell phone connection. My day just continued downhill and I seemed to be the cause of it.

I advised the Coast Guard of our position and status regarding weather, seas, fuel, etc. I informed them of my ETA to Tarpon Springs and we agreed to make a radio check every half hour with them. Everyone was ok and we continued on in the total black taking waves over our starboard side. Filing a float plan with my mother-in-law paid off and it was a great feeling to know people were watching out for us.

The time finally came when I had to add fuel to the main tank, so I had Kathy take the helm and I proceeded to empty the additional fuel cans into the tanks. It was a very tricky process in the howling wind and high seas, but we were successful and continued on our way.

As we neared Alcote Key located off the entrance to Tarpon Springs I decided that with the severe seas increasing I would tuck in behind the key, out of the wind. If we could not make it through the shoals we would anchor for the night in the shelter of the key and head in the following morning.

With some tricky maneuvering I managed to work our way through the shoals and into the river at which time we received the next stroke of bad luck for the night. We had made it down the entire coast in the dark through the crab pot area known as the "Mine Field" without a problem. Now as I entered the navigation channel to Tarpon Springs I picked up a crab pot around my port prop and had to shut down the port engine. I decided that since we were so close to our destination that we would just limp our way up the river.

Well, we did it; we finally made it into Tarpon Springs and headed to our reserved slip. Sure enough, one final problem for the night, some other boat was in our slip and the Marina was closed. There was no one around the Marina that we could call for assistance. Now what? I had finally had enough and decided to tie up at the sponge boat dock across the river and worry about the marina in the morning. Kathy took Deedee for a much needed walk ashore and then we crashed for the night. All is well that ends well, or so they tell me.

FEAR KNOT

I didn't sleep all that well, soaked in fuel and saltwater, but at least we were safe and in port. That is what really counts after an experience like this. I guess the real reason I didn't sleep that well is because I kept thinking that if I had followed my own rules none of this would have happened. I've learned a big lesson over the last 24 hours. So this whole incident does have an upside to it and it will not happen again.

The following morning we contacted the marina and they cleared our slip so we could get secured. Kathy's parents drove down from New Port Richey, all is well and everyone is smiling. I was also able to contact a local diver who came over and removed the crab pot from the prop, so we were in full service again. Not only had we made it, but we had made it in time and had a wonderful Thanksgiving dinner compliments of my mother-in-law.

It was time to take a break for the holidays! We were able to celebrate Thanksgiving with Kathy's parents and enjoy some much needed time together. Over the next few days I got the boat prepared to stay tied up for awhile, as we were going to fly back to Wisconsin for Christmas and time with the family. The first phase of our journey has been just awesome and I can't wait to continue.

GENE SCHNAGL

PHOTOS

Tarpon Springs sponge fishing docks

Tide is out at Tarpon Springs

Tarpon Springs sunset

FEAR KNOT

Diver removing crab pot from prop

Crab pot remains from the prop

GENE SCHNAGL

The crew at Longboat Key

Longboat Key shore leave

Looper crew members on shore leave

FEAR KNOT

Northern Gulf ICW

Gulf of Mexico marker

Tied up at Captiva Island

GENE SCHNAGL

CHAPTER 11 – THE FLORIDA GULF COAST

Returning to Wisconsin for the Holidays with the family was great, but I was getting anxious to get back to the boat. It was then I came up with an idea to make this trip that much better for all of us. I decided to go to Sea School to obtain my Captain's License. I was aware of a new class starting in New Port Richey, Florida. So I signed up immediately.

We discussed my idea and agreed, so Kathy was able to stay in Wisconsin our daughter and grandson for awhile, while I attended the class. I stayed on the boat and used some of my spare time to service the engines, etc. I used our scooter to get back and forth to classes in New Port Richey and it worked great. The school was very intense, but I learned more about boating than I ever thought I would know. It was well worth the time spent and will pay off in making our journey much more enjoyable. I enjoyed it so much that after getting my 6-Pack Captain's License I made plans for returning to Sea School to obtain my Master's License. I would definitely recommend this to all Captains planning on doing America's Great Loop. The education proved to be extremely valuable.

ANXIETY FACTOR – *I'm not confident that I have the necessary skills to safely Captain our boat on this challenging of a cruise. How can I gain the confidence I feel I need?*

Most Captains tend to be a little over confident at times and if they are the least bit unsure they will try not to let others see this. Normally this works ok for them, but I would recommend that because of the many new issues and challenges involved in this type of cruise that you be open and discuss these concerns with your partner. She/he will be just as much at risk as you during this voyage.

Try to identify what both your concerns are and list them for discussion. I think that you will find that most of them can be taken care of just through planning with experienced Loopers at an AGLCA Rendezvous or through the AGLCA online discussion sites.

I would also recommend that, if you have not already, you should both attend some boating classes with organizations such as the Power Squadron or the Coast Guard Auxiliary

If you have the opportunity I would also seriously recommend that you attend a Sea School and obtain your Captain's License. This level of training is designed for professional Captains and will provide you with knowledge at a commercial boating level and remember you will be meeting many commercial vessels along your journey. Knowing in advance what that commercial Captain is thinking can help you avoid many difficult situations and is a tremendous boost to your confidence and that of your crew.

Day 133 – February 13, 2006, Kathy returned to Tarpon Springs today. With her is our new crew, our daughter Katie and her infant son, Max. They will be cruising with us for a short time and then will fly back home again. There are some fun times ahead and I can't wait to weigh anchor.

Day 137 – Well I did it, I spent all last Wednesday at the U.S. Coast Guard Station in Tampa Bay taking my Captain's Test. I was able to complete the entire test in one day and passed it the first time so I now am a licensed Captain. I feel smarter, but we'll have to wait and see to find out if there have been any changes for the better. My crew tells me I don't look any smarter, but what do they know, they think water is for drinking.

After completing the testing and getting the crew settled in, we bid Kathy's parents farewell and headed south again. There was a short wait for the tide to come in, to get enough water under us, and then we stopped at the fuel dock to top off. We will be working our way down the coast toward Tampa Bay for our first stop.

We decided to spend the night at the Gulf Harbor Marina at Boca Ciega before crossing Tampa Bay. It is a scenic and secluded marina off the ICW and we spent a pleasant evening on board just relaxing.

The next morning as we headed into Tampa Bay we hit a solid wall of fog. Tampa Bay is a wide, shallow body of water with heavy shipping so crossing in clear weather takes a lot of attention. It was now time for an instrument crossing using radar, chart plotter and good observation and hearing by the crew. I headed east up the North Channel toward the Sunshine Bridge and then turned south to cross the bay. You couldn't see a thing except on radar and you could hear the traffic on the bridge above you but we made the crossing and I then turned west to locate a channel marker near the ICW again. I was able to hit the marker dead on and we then turned south again into the ICW. Sure enough, the fog lifted as soon as we left the Bay and my white knuckles got their color back quickly.

ANXIETY FACTOR – We've heard that fog and other boaters can be a problem in Florida waters, is this true?

Fog is going to be expected on any of the waters you will be cruising. The best suggestion is to wait until the fog lifts and then head out. Fog will come and go most mornings with the sun coming up.

If you must travel in fog being prepared to carefully watch your instruments and keeping lookouts posted at all times is a must.

Personal experience has shown me that local boaters in the Florida waters are many and seem to be unaware of exactly what the boating safety rules are. Watch out for them and always assume they will not be doing what they should be doing. I found they do not use lights or sound devices in heavy fog and will continue to run at high speed under zero visibility conditions. Should you find yourself in this type of situation be extra alert and sound your fog warnings to warn them you are out there. Also watch for crab pots and unlit markers in the fog. Again, best rule is to wait in a safe area until the fog lifts and then proceed on.

The rest of the day was a beautiful cruise and we made it to our destination at the Marina on Longboat Key. Along the way a few dolphins joined us and we enjoyed the company although I'm not sure Max ever figured out exactly what they were. We had previously made arrangements to meet up again with some friends we met coming down the rivers and were planning a spending a few days at Longboat Key with them. The Marina is beautiful and my crew enjoyed the swimming pool and the sun as well as the excellent dining and shopping on the Key.

After a few days it was time for my new crew to depart and fly back to Wisconsin. We drove

them to the airport in Tampa and they headed home as we prepared to push on south. We will miss them and look forward to seeing them again soon. And, yes, there were a few tears shed during the goodbyes.

The following day we awoke to heavy fog again so we waited for the lift and about 10:00am started south. Naturally the fog settled back in again so we spent our time crossing Sarasota Bay dodging crab pots, jet skies with no lights, and fishermen with no lights, etc. This is where electronics become a necessity. And again, most of the jet skis and small fishing boats do not have radios, or don't turn them on, so you can't call them and warn them to be careful. Use that horn to let them know you are there. Keep in mind that you can see them but they can't see you.

ANXIETY FACTOR – *If we don't want to do The Loop alone should we invite others to join us?*

Most Loopers invite other family or friends to join them on their cruise. Not only is it fun to have family or friends along, it can also cut the expenses down. Many friends will cruise for a section of the Loop and share expenses along the way. They will then catch a flight home and new friends will fly in for the next section, again sharing expenses.

Adding friends and family also gives you additional crew for handling lines in locks or while docking while in heavy winds as well as easing that little bit of home sickness that may set in now and then. Don't hesitate to invite others to join you.

After a day of sunshine we docked at the Crow's Nest Marina in Venice, Florida. It was a great location and we relaxed and enjoyed watching all the boats coming in off the Gulf. After dinner at the Crow's Nest we got things ready for our shove off in the morning to Captiva Island.

The run from Venice to Captiva is only about forty miles on the Gulf ICW. The weather was beautiful and the water calm. The only problem was the fact that it was Saturday and a million day boaters were out on the ICW going every direction. Naturally, I had to meet the one that didn't know you never drive on the wrong side of the ICW in a little boat heading straight at a very big boat. The operator wasn't totally sober and I finally had to go aground to avoid a collision which damaged my starboard prop as I went aground on a shoal. I was able to rock the boat off the shoal and we limped our way down to the Tween Waters Marina on Captiva Island. I didn't think the damage was too serious and at least there hadn't been a collision. It was interesting to note that as the other boat went by I could overhear his passenger ask him, "what are all those red and green floats for?" to which he responded, "oh don't worry, those are for those big boats." I now knew why he was on the wrong side of the ICW.

Being a certified SCUBA diver I had prepared for our trip by having a Hookah diving outfit on board. Hookah is a form of diving that allows one to breathe through a hose attached to an air compressor on board your vessel. I had planned on diving to check our damage once we reached Captiva, but due to a dockside leg injury I was unable to dive so I had my brother come over from Cape Coral, Florida to make the dive for me. He was unable to determine any severe damage so we decided to have the boat lifted out for repair when we reached Fort Myers Beach, our next planned port of call.

The next day we headed out and made our way to Fort Myers Beach Marina. The following morning we had the boat lifted out and found that the starboard prop was bent and that is what was causing the vibration. I decided to leave it for now as the Marina could not handle the work for a week or more and we would push on to Centennial Marina at Fort Myers where we intended to stay for some time. I would hire a diver to pull the prop, have it tuned and then replaced and we would be all set again.

The following morning we headed out and up the Caloosahatchee River and pulled into Centennial Marina. As I neared the docks I heard a call on the VHF radio stating, "Del Coronado, is that you?" We were back together again with some of our friends we had made up on the Tennessee River. It was going to be a great time in Florida.

CHAPTER 12 – WINTER IN FLORIDA

We had finally reached the marina where we had planned on taking a winter break and doing a little land cruising. Centennial Marina was a great location and we rented a car to get around in. A lot of boating "Snowbirds" keep their boats here and we were making a lot of new friends.

Our original plan had been moving on later to the Keys and then to the Dry Tortugas, over to the Bahamas and then up the east coast. As nothing is ever written in stone, our plans changed. While home over the holidays, Kathy had found an opportunity to buy a jewelry store and that opportunity was coming to fruition. What can I say; I am married to a gemologist.

We decided to spend about a month where we were to explore Florida and then head over the Lake Okeechobee route to allow us to complete the Loop. That would put us home by September which was when Kathy hoped to open the new store.

Between sightseeing and having fun I will be doing some charting so it will keep me busy. I'll just have to plan another cruise to see the other areas I cut out. I've kept the charts for the Dry Tortugas and Bahamas as they will be used at a later date.

Staying put for awhile is a great idea. It allowed us to relax with many friends. It also allowed me some serious time to work on the boat and resupply. It gave Kathy some great "girl" time with the other gals which she needed after a long cruise. I'm really glad that we decided to do this to take some of the travel pressure off of us.

Day 180 – Well, it's April 2nd and we are finally on our way again. We will head east up the Caloosahatchee River and work our way toward something we haven't seen in awhile, locks. We will be back in the locks again so Kathy is getting ready to get her hands a little dirty. This first day we will hit three locks which will take us up to Lake Okeechobee and the town of Morehaven, Florida.

We were planning on heading straight through to Roland Martin Marina in Clewston, Florida, but I developed an engine miss and decided to stay at Morehaven to check things out. While Kathy talked with some of the local gals and walked Deedee I found that I had a little water in a fuel filter so a quick change and we were ready to go again. Meeting the great people we met in Morehaven I'm kind of glad we had the little engine problem. It's a nice, friendly stop.

In the morning we headed down the west shoreline of Lake Okeechobee. There is not a lot to see except for swamp along this area. Even swamp is scenic when you are on the water.

The water level is up so the lock into Roland Martin's was just left open. It's a very popular stop and we had a fun evening with the local fishing crowd. In the morning we will cross Lake Okeechobee.

Crossing the Lake was very relaxing. The lake was calm with moderate boat traffic during the crossing. It didn't seem that long and we arrived at our destination of Port Mayaca on the east shore. With the high water the lock was again left open and we headed straight through toward our next port of call, Indian Town Marina, where we would be spending the night. It was a very calm canal type ride, but with a lot of boat traffic in the canal.

ANXIETY FACTOR – *Are there any special concerns regarding crossing Lake Okeechobee?*

Lake Okeechobee is a wide but extremely shallow lake. There are two crossing routes. One is mid-lake and the other is following the south shoreline. Mid-lake will usually provide the best water depth conditions but the route changes course frequently and the markers are spaced out at long distances. Just be sure to follow your headings carefully as you cross. Also be sure, as always, to check the weather before beginning your crossing. Have your lookout stay alert for other boat traffic as you cross, as it can get a little heavy this time of year. Many boaters are beginning their migration north again. Most boats must be out of Florida waters and into the north before July for insurance purposes, due to hurricane season coming later in the summer.

<u>ANXIETY FACTOR</u> – When leaving Ft. Myers to cross Lake Okeechobee are there any fuel issues?

There are a number of fuel stops along the way from Ft. Myers all the way to St. Lucie. We had checked before we left Ft. Myers, but found out on the way that most were closed or were out of fuel due to heavy boat traffic. If fuel might be a concern for you, just make sure to call ahead before planning on stopping at a certain location. The same applies for marinas. Due to the heavy boat traffic many marinas are full this time of year, so be sure to call ahead for reservations if you plan to stay at a certain location.

FEAR KNOT

PHOTOS

Checking prop damage at Captiva Island

Relaxing at Captiva Island

Centennial Marina at Ft.Myers, Florida

Caloosahatchee River up bound at Ft. Myers, Florida

Be careful what you tie up to when the tides in

FEAR KNOT

Morehaven Marina on Lake Okeechobee

Lake Okeechobee anchorage

Lake Okeechobee west shoreline

Lake Okeechobee high water open locks

Relaxing on the docks at Roland Martin's Marina, Lake Okeechobee

Setting charts for crossing Lake Okeechobee while relaxing at Roland Martin's Marina

Beautiful St. Augustine, Florida lighthouse

GENE SCHNAGL

CHAPTER 13 – NORTHWARD BOUND

After spending the night at Indian Town Marina we headed out in the morning in route to Vero Beach, Fl, where we would be northward bound again. Our first stop on the way was the St. Lucie Lock. We had a short wait for the lock but then we were on our way. I noticed that we were back in saltwater and that it was getting clearer and that light green color again. It wasn't long and we made our turn up the east coast ICW. It's been quite awhile since we've been headed north. Upon arriving at Vero Beach we decided to go just a short distance north to Loggerhead Marina and spend the night there. Another beautiful Florida day is behind us.

Day 184 – Today we plan on making a little longer run to Titusville, FL, or as it is called, Space City. The boat traffic is very heavy on the ICW so we have to make a lot of passes, but I am staying polite and slowing down to no wake for each one. I just wish some of the sport fishing boats would do the same, as they are really rocking the small craft and sailboats. Where is the water patrol when you really need them?

As we cruised along I noticed a vessel ahead of me that looked familiar from the stern and I grabbed the binoculars to get a better view. Sure enough, we had caught up with some friends, and Loopers, we had last seen on the Tennessee River. All these miles and we were back together again. I called them on the radio and we decided to get together again for dinner in Daytona Beach in a couple of days. Kathy got on the phone and made slip and dinner reservations for both of us so we were all set. What a great surprise.

We arrived at Titusville Marina where we were spending the night. We were directly across from the Kennedy Space Center, but unfortunately there was no launch scheduled. Kathy had a great time finding fresh strawberries for sale nearby. She almost made herself sick with strawberries and a small bowl of sugar. It was a wonderful treat and the Admiral had earned it! She enjoyed her find and I relaxed and caught up on the blog and my charts. We spent another wonderful evening relaxing after a beautiful 65 mile run.

Day 185 – We are on our way to Daytona Beach on another sunshine filled day. Again, lots of boat traffic but we are moving along just fine at about 9-11 knots. Slow and easy and enjoying the scenery.

FEAR KNOT

In the late morning I noticed another small sailboat ahead and notified them by radio that I would be making a slow pass on their starboard side. As we came alongside, I saw that it was the couple of Canadian ladies again, we had not seen since the Tennessee River. I guess everyone is on the move. It was great to see them again and I slowed so Kathy could talk to them for a few minutes. We then wished them smooth seas and continued on our way.

Later in the early afternoon I entered a small channel cut through a key on the ICW. About half way through I saw a lot of commotion in the water ahead of me and had to come to a stop as I couldn't figure out what was going on. There, in the channel, was a pod of about six manatees playing and having a ball rolling around in the water. As other boats were approaching I warned them on the radio and we all stopped to watch the show for about ten minutes, then off they went, on their way. What a great experience.

We later arrived at Daytona Beach Marina and got settled in. It wasn't too long and here came our boating friends we had met the day before. After some boat cleaning and crew cleaning we relaxed with a cocktail and then caught a cab to a recommended restaurant. It was a great dinner and evening with great Looper friends.

The following morning we said goodbye to our friends and headed north again with a destination of St. Augustine, Florida. The plan is to spend a couple of days there sightseeing and getting caught up on some calls to home. We are both looking forward to the break.

The day was a short cruising day but tiring. We had very high winds and heavy traffic so conditions required a lot of concentration on my part. The ICW is also shallow along this run with lots of twists and turns. Shoaling can be a problem so we had to pay close attention to the charts and markers while fighting the wind so we didn't get blown aground. Still it beat a day at work, right?

We finally made it to our destination, the Anchorage Inn and Marina on Anastasia Island, located next to the Lion's Bridge crossing to St. Augustine.

As tomorrow is the Blessing of the fleet at St. Augustine, we decided to stay and take part in the festival. This is a wonderful port with so much history that we are looking forward to our stay. I unloaded the motor scooter and we started our adventure into history.

ANXIETY FACTOR – *If we need supplies are there many locations to get them along the waterways?*

Naturally, there are always stores at the ports and many marinas have courtesy cars for boaters staying at the marina. Some of the smaller stores can have higher prices but at least you can get what you need. The best location we found for picking up supplies is the Wal-Mart Superstore. It seemed that every larger town along the way had one. Many times we could pick up everything we needed to restock. Kathy and I would get a haircut and Kathy would get her nails done. I even got my glasses repaired at one. Resupply is just not a problem.

After a few wonderful days in St. Augustine we had decided we had better move on. Besides that, the weather had turned and the winds were really blowing. We had a lot of rain, but with a break in the wind we thought it best to move on.

ANXIETY FACTOR – Do the tides, currents, winds, etc. propose a problem on the Atlantic ICW?

For inland boaters the tidal waters can take a little getting used to but are not really that difficult. We found that in ports such as St. Augustine where the ocean access is right at the port, things can get a little tricky. With wind, a tide change and strong currents, you want to be very aware of their affect on your vessel and be prepared to adjust quickly. With a little practice you will find yourself adjusting without really thinking about it. The main thing is being aware that you have strong currents with tidal changes and being prepared for them.

We had no sooner started out and the winds came back up. So much for the marine weather

report! The problem was constant 20-30 knot winds all day long. By mid afternoon I had had enough. At Jacksonville Beach we were able to obtain a slip at the Palm Cove Marina and called it a day. Lucky for us there was no boat traffic due to the high winds so it was an easy day that way, but I was pretty burned out from fighting the weather conditions.

Our plan is to clean all the salt spray off the boat in the morning and just call it a day. We had hoped to leave the following day but the severe weather continued so we stayed put and made some new friends. That's what marinas are for, right?

In the morning the weather broke and we headed out. Our plan is to make another long run of about 65 miles to Jekyll Island, Georgia. The day was a smooth run, with the only water to worry about were the inlets off the Atlantic, and their high winds and currents. The currents and tides can do a little twist and pull on you but you get used to it quickly and just adjust.

We arrived at Jekyll Island Marina, but I had come in on low tide and the water was very thin. I had to tie up on the outside of the face dock, as there was nothing but mud on the inside. I was churning mud as it was, so that night I cleaned my sea strainers just to be on the safe side. I'll be paying closer attention to the tides tomorrow when we leave.

In the morning as we headed north again I heard a radio call from a boat that had been tied up overnight in front of us. I guess he had left early and was traveling pretty fast when he missed a temporary marker and ran high aground on a new shoal. I, later with the aid of some other large boats, tried to rock him off the shoal with waves, but he had gone too far in. He had to call for a tow to get him off so we continued on our way.

ANXIETY FACTOR – *Do we have to be concerned about the water depth along the ICW?*

Most of the ICW is kept pretty well dredged by the Army Corp of Engineers. There are a couple of states that do have some depth concerns. Georgia does not always seem to have the dredging done when needed and the shoaling can change very quickly. Many times the channel markers are in place but the shoal has extended out into the channel and a small temporary buoy is set. Be sure to watch for temporary buoys, listen to the radio chatter and keep yourself aware of grounding reports. Also, take it slow as you travel so if you do go aground you don't drive yourself too far onto the shoal, which may allow you to back right off again.

The other state we found a problem with is New Jersey. Another state you may want to consider traveling outside along the coast whenever water and weather conditions are right. It could save you a lot of clogged sea strainers and maybe a tow or two.

GENE SCHNAGL

PHOTOS

Travel buddies on the ICW

Stirring up food for the Terns in the shallow ICW

Playing manatees blocked our way for awhile in the channel

FEAR KNOT

Crew and her ball on shore leave

Beautiful Georgia savannahs

Walking to dinner on a Georgia country road

Our next stop was Kilkenny Creek Marina; a classic southern marina set off about a mile and a half from the ICW in the waterway savannahs a little south of Savannah, Georgia. It was a little tricky finding the channel amidst all the tall savannah grass but well worth it for a great taste of boating in the south.

After cleaning the boat we walked about a quarter mile up a quaint country road, lined with huge oak trees draped in Spanish moss, to a local country restaurant. I probably don't need to mention this, but the catfish dinner was totally awesome. The local people were super friendly and just wanted to talk about our boating adventure. It was a truly pleasant evening.

As we walked back, the real "south" hit us, the mosquitoes had found us, so we walked a little faster and then settled in for some well needed rest. I have to say though that the sunset over the savannahs is something you will never forget and is stunning.

In the morning we woke to another sunny day. A surprise came when I went up on deck and found that our white boat was now a black. The entire boat was covered with black sand gnats. These are nasty, mean little critters, which love to bite so we shoved off as quickly as we could and headed out into the ICW. I decided I would clean the boat later when we reached Savannah, Georgia.

After cruising up the ICW about forty miles we turned up the Savannah River and later tied up at the Savannah Georgia City Dock. A beautiful location right at the center of the Savannah historical district with easy walking access to everything you want to see. Shortly after our arrival our friends from Jacksonville, Florida arrived and we set off sightseeing and spent a great afternoon and evening enjoying the beautiful port.

Easter Sunday – Today we left beautiful Savannah, Georgia and started north again. Happy Easter! We were now in South Carolina and our destination was Beaufort, South Carolina. Along the way we passed Hilton Head Island but decided not to stop as we had visited there in the past. The weather was great but hot with the temperature in the 90's. It felt great on the water as usual, with a light breeze.

With all the heavy boat traffic the marinas are filling up quickly so we called ahead and got a reservation at the Lady's Island Marina on the coast side of the ICW. We got the boat washed down; the crew showered and sat on the aft deck in the shade enjoying a cold drink, watching all the boat traffic with a cool breeze off the water. Life is still very good!

Being a good Captain and husband, I decided to treat Kathy for Easter Sunday. I made dinner and prepared ham, scalloped potatoes, corn and homemade biscuits. Who says you can't live well on a boat? She wasn't even aware I had picked up all the goodies that last time we went shopping. What's a boat without a good galley, right?

ANXIETY FACTOR – *I understand navigational markers but I've heard that on the ICW you can sometimes find markers that have both red and green panels on them. This really sounds confusing. What do I do if I see one of these?*

Yes, you will find this sometimes on the ICW. This is caused as a result of two waterways converging at one point. An example would be if you were northbound on the ICW on the Atlantic coast then green would be on your right. As you met with an inlet from the Atlantic then red would be on your right if you were coming in from the sea. Just keep in mind which waterway you are following.

We departed Beaufort, South Carolina and are making a sixty mile run to Charleston, South Carolina. Kathy has a sister in Raleigh, North Carolina and she and her family will be driving down to spend a few days with us. It will be a fun break with a lot of sightseeing and I think we are ready for a little family time again.

FEAR KNOT

We arrived at Charleston Bay and proceeded to cross the bay. To accomplish this it required that we go out to Fort Sumter in the South channel and then turn back into the bay in the North Channel. The middle of Charleston Bay is extremely shallow and shoaled so it's best to go around; follow your charts carefully.

We then tied up at the Hilton Charleston Harbor Marina with the retired aircraft carrier, U.S.S. Yorktown, anchored directly behind us. Of course they had a much bigger slip than we did.

After a few days of family sightseeing, Kathy's sister and her family headed back to Raleigh and we got ready to move on. Some foul weather was coming in so we decided to wait it out one more day and then shove off.

The weather finally cleared with only 20-25 knot winds remaining so we decided to push on. It wasn't long until we found out that South Carolina had also not completed much of the ICW dredging and going became extremely slow and cautious. Along our route passing was very slow and there was a lot of boat traffic. We came upon one large trawler and one large motor yacht both hard aground where the charts indicated channel but shoaling had occurred and the temporary markers were not out yet. Again, it was a matter of going slow and watching for water depth changes.

We successfully completed our 60 mile run and arrived at Georgetown Landing Marina in Georgetown, South Carolina. After fueling up we tied up, washed down the boat, showered the crew and called it a day. Again, it was time to take Deedee for some play time ashore and just relax a little. In the morning we will head on up to Myrtle Beach, South Carolina to spend a couple of days ashore with the scooter again and do some exploring.

Day 201 – We are on our way to Myrtle Beach. When I say we, I mean we, the crew, and thousands of the worst biting flies I have ever seen. We were lucky that we had insect repellent on board and Kathy broke it out fast. It is a fantastic product and all the biting stopped even though the flies were still with us. Kathy started with the fly swatter to keep busy and she smacked hundreds of them. After awhile she decided to dump the "bodies" overboard, but when she looked to the deck there were none. I almost didn't have the heart to tell her that Deedee thought it was snack time and as fast as they hit the deck she lapped them up. I thought it was pretty funny, but I will skip the conversation my crew had with me at this point. (Trust me; it really was funny to watch!)

Even with the flies, which eventually disappeared, the stretch of water to Myrtle Beach is very scenic. The scenery is incredible and just kept getting better.

South of Myrtle Beach you approach a marked area known as "The Rocks." You will have to use caution in this area and be sure to stay in the channel. The sides are large rocks and are unforgiving so be careful.

ANXIETY FACTOR – Is the area south of Myrtle Beach, South Carolina called "The Rocks" as dangerous as I've heard?

The Rocks area is not necessarily dangerous but it does require a lot of alertness and caution. It is an area about five miles long where the shorelines are covered with large boulders which can cause a lot of damage. Also, the channel is very narrow. So narrow that should you meet an approaching tow with barges you will have to turn around and go back to the closest side channel to allow it to pass before you can continue. Watch your depth carefully; stay alert on the radio with lookouts posted and all should be fine.

GENE SCHNAGL

PHOTOS

He went hard aground in Georgia ICW

Passing traffic on the Savannah River

Tied up at Savannah, Georgia

FEAR KNOT

Beautiful Georgia sunset

Combating the South Carolina biting flies

Passing through the "Rocks" at Myrtle Beach

GENE SCHNAGL

ICW live fire area, Camp LaJeune, South Carolina

Charleston, South Carolina Marina

Caution! ICW dredging

Cruising past Fort Sumter, South Carolina

Daytona Beach Marina, Florida

After traveling about fifty miles we arrived at the beautiful Coquina Yacht Club where we had made reservations. It was a beautiful place to stay. This is located in the same harbor as the Myrtle Beach Yacht Club. It was so nice we decided to unload the scooter again and spend a few days exploring, which we greatly enjoyed. Myrtle Beach is a great area to spend some time. Not only did we get a lot of exploring done, but I had a chance to get the boat cleaned up and polish some isinglass. The marina manager was such a great gal, she took Kathy shopping with her, showed her where to get her nails done and then picked her up to bring her back to the Marina.

Day 210 – After a few relaxing days we loaded up and headed north to North Carolina. No sooner had we crossed the state line than the skies opened up and a wall of water came down on us. We knew we were supposed to get some rain but not like this. The winds picked up to about 30 knots. And visibility dropped to zero with the rain coming down so hard, that for safety reasons, we decided to call it a day and pulled into a small marina in the town of Southport, North Carolina. The winds were coming so fast we decided to leave the boat on a face dock rather than a slip and the marina manager agreed.

FEAR KNOT

It looked like this weather was going to last a couple of days so we are going to ride it out there. With a restaurant just across the road from the marina we should be just fine.

After two days of rain, it finally let up and we decided to proceed. We hadn't traveled that far when the winds suddenly picked up to around 30 knots again and a lot of boats were having trouble staying under control in the narrow ICW. For safety we decided to call it a day and pulled into the Snead's Ferry Marina in Snead's Ferry, North Carolina. The marina wasn't the prettiest marina you have ever seen, but it had a solid dock. Immediately after us a number of boats also pulled in for protection from the high winds. As I walked around the marina I noticed all the local slips had grills made from 50 gallon drums cut in half and old rusted out vans parked next to the slips. I guess you could call the area "rustic."

With the winds not letting up for two days we decided to head to town. We met another stranded couple on a sailboat from Detroit, Michigan and asked them to join us in the courtesy car from the marina and we all headed to Jacksonville, North Carolina, the nearest big town. We had lunch at a nice restaurant, took in a movie at the local theater and then caught up on some shopping to resupply. It was a great day with great people.

After a couple of days we decided to move on with the improved weather, so off we went. I should point out here that you may not know of Snead's Ferry but you may have heard of it by its other name, Camp LaJeune. One of the largest Marine Corp bases you will ever see. It made for an interesting stay with the Helicopter gunships flying over day and night and the booms from the base cannon fire. I would wake up in the night thinking I was back in the Army again. Maybe that is what they mean when they say "white noise" can help you sleep.

ANXIETY FACTOR – ARE THERE ANY RESTRICTED AREAS ALONG THE ICW?

There are some controlled areas you must be aware of on the Atlantic ICW. One of these is just south of Charleston, South Carolina Harbor. There is a nuclear submarine base in this area. As we approached the area I saw a nuclear submarine approaching us and a couple of navy gunboats nearby. I radioed and asked if they wanted me to hold position as I could see that they had not observed that I was approaching. After their surprise of finding I was right behind them they stated yes hold position which I did and one of the gunboats stayed in front of us until the submarine had passed and cleared. We were then advised that we could proceed on our way. Just a little caution here, try not to surprise a U.S. Navy gunboat, they get a little nervous.

Another area is at Camp LaJeune where they perform live fire over the ICW. If they are firing you must wait until you are cleared to proceed. Pay attention to the signs located along the ICW. You may find that gunboats will block your passage until safe to continue. Just follow their directions.

All these areas are marked on your charts and in your waterway guides. Be alert and remember to maintain your mandatory safety distances from all war ships. You should not have any issues in these areas by being alert and observant.

After clearing the "live fire" area we had a nice smooth day of cruising. We finally reached Bogue Sound, a fifteen mile long sound that we will be crossing. This was the reason I did not depart a day earlier in the high winds in anticipation of having to cross all this open water. Today the water was just great with about 10 knot winds and we had smooth cruising.

<u>*ANXIETY FACTOR*</u> *– What should I be looking for as I plan my cruise for the next day?*

Besides picking the distance you want to travel the next day and where you want to anchor or slip for the night, you will want to look over the details of your Waterway Guides and Charts. Check the Waterway Guides for recommendations and advisories. Check your weather forecasts and determine if you have any large open bodies of water you will have to cross where wind, etc. might have an adverse affect on you. Check your Marina Alerts for any special information for the areas you will be cruising in.

Keep in mind that even though you are in the protected waters of the ICW as you enter sounds you will be exposed to conditions offshore that could compromise your safety. Do your research the night before and the morning of departure. Stay alert to Marine advisories while under way and you should have safe cruising.

After cruising Bogue Sound we arrived at Morehead City, North Carolina and pulled into our slip at the Morehead Yacht Basin where we had a reservation for the evening. A quick wash of the boat to get the salt off, play time with the dog and we called it a day. With Wi-Fi at the marina I decided to get some office time in on the blog so I relaxed on the aft deck and Kathy relaxed with a book. This is what boating is all about! I also got some next day chart work in as we were planning a long 70 mile run tomorrow. We'll see how it goes in the morning.

We set out the next morning knowing that we were going to have to run some open water again, but the winds were down so the cruising should be easy. It wasn't long and we entered into the Neuse River. We continued north until we hit a turn marker and then headed northwest up the Bay River and traveled inland until coming out at Pamlico River where we were back in open water again.

Crossing Pamlico requires that you watch your charts as you will have a mid course change in the center of the river which is about three miles out. At that point we changed course and headed north up the Pungo River to our destination at the Belhaven Marina at Belhaven, North Carolina.

At the marina we refueled and then cleaned the ever present salt off the boat. Deedee had her play time and then Kathy and I decided to take the marina courtesy car to town for dinner. The courtesy car turned out to be an electric golf cart with no brakes. It worked just fine driving down Main Street, but was a little awkward when I had to drag my foot to stop at the traffic light. We even stopped next to the town police car and the Officer just smiled and waved to us as I dragged to a stop. Lots of friendly people here in Belhaven and the dinners were excellent.

When we shoved off in the morning we headed east and then turned north into the Alligator River-Pungo River Canal which was taking us north and east again. This is a manmade canal that was taking us to the Alligator River. We then continued up the river until arriving at the Alligator River Marina at Columbia, North Carolina.

After fueling and cleaning the boat we saw our sailboat friends from Detroit, Michigan pulling into the marina. It was great to see them again after such a long time. They got settled in and we all went to dinner at the marina restaurant. I must say that this is one of the cleanest marinas I have ever seen and it was great staying there. Loopers always hear the tales of "Wicked Wanda" on America's Great Loop. Well, Wanda is the owner/operator of the Alligator River Marina. I found Wanda to be a super friendly and knowledgeable gal who just speaks her mind when she has to. Ok, maybe even if she doesn't have to, but if you meet Wanda just smile and you will get a big smile in return.

I checked the weather carefully that night and everything looked good for the next day. We were going to be running the length of Albemarle Sound and it would be a lot of open water with a million crab pots along the way.

In the morning the skies were clear and it was nice and warm so off we went. It wasn't long and we were in the open water dodging crab pots. Kathy watched the port side from center and I watched the starboard side from center and we avoided them all. By mid afternoon we arrived at our destination of Elizabeth City, North Carolina.

ANXIETY FACTOR – *I have heard that crab pots are a real hazard and can cause you lots of problems on the ICW?*

You are going to run into crab pots anywhere you go along the coasts. I would not call them a hazard but you must constantly be aware of them. They are not supposed to be set in navigation channels, but they do set them right along the edges. By doing this they sometimes get blown into the channels and can be a problem for you. The pot floats are also often colors that are difficult to see on the water such as green, blue, black, etc.

If you divide your watch areas like Kathy and I did where she watches from bow center to port and you watch from bow center to starboard it works very well to avoid them. Have your lookout use their binoculars and you just stay alert.

Arriving at Elizabeth City Marina is quite an experience. It is called America's Friendliest city and the Rose City. The Marina slips are free to all boaters although there is no electrical hookup. There is also a free wine and cheese party every evening to allow the boaters to socialize with the locals and each other. You will find that when you are tied up, a gentleman called the Rose buddy will pull up in a golf cart and request to see the "Admiral." He is not interested in talking to the Captains. He will present her with a long stem rose, welcome her to Elizabeth City and invite you to the cheese and wine party that evening. It just doesn't get any friendlier than that.

This port was so nice we decided to stay an extra day to explore the quaint community. It

was well worth the extra time and was a lot of fun.

Day 215 – After a wonderful couple of days we thought we had best move on as we were now going to cruise the Dismal Swamp, a stretch of water we had heard so much about and were really looking forward to. By taking this route we not only got to cruise a piece of history, but it saved having to go off shore into the Atlantic and around and back into Chesapeake Bay and Norfolk, Virginia. *NOT TRUE*

The Dismal Swamp was a canal with locks on either end that began construction in 1764 through financing by General George Washington and other investors. It is a fascinating piece of history to enjoy as a boater. As it is a closed water system the water is fresh water and not salt.

After saying goodbye to the wonderful people at the Elizabeth City Marina we cruised about 18 miles upriver to the first lock.

We had timed it just right as the lock only opens four times a day and we made the 11:00am opening with one other sailboat and locked right through. We were now in fresh water again. As our boat has raw water engine intakes this worked great for flushing out the system. I even started the generator to flush that system out as well.

It is one of the most scenic and beautiful waterways you will ever encounter and we just slowly cruised our way along with the many small local vessels in the canal.

ANXIETY FACTOR – *I've heard that the Dismal Swamp has a lot of stumps and can cause damage to your prop, is this true?*

The Dismal Swamp canal is about 35 miles long and it is "No Wake" the entire length. As it was dug through a cypress swamp there are many stumps on the bottom that could be struck by a deep draft vessel such as a sailboat with a deep keel. During our entire cruise I experienced one minor tick which caused no damage whatsoever. The key is to stay to the center of the channel and avoid going toward the shorelines as much as possible. You will be traveling at no wake speed so you should have very little problem. Just enjoy the absolute beauty of the course you are on and watch your depth.

We completed our journey down the Dismal Swamp and arrived at the second lock at Deep Creek, Virginia. We had to wait for a lock opening so we tied up with two other boats. It was then we noticed one of the boats was from Canada and was crewed by friends we had made in Myrtle Beach, South Carolina where we had last seen them. We made plans to get together again as we headed north.

When the lock opened we entered and got tied up. While waiting Kathy noticed the huge number of conch shells all around the gardens at the lock house. One of the Lock Masters approached our boat and asked Kathy if we had a blowing conch on board and she responded that we did. He asked her to please get it and hand it to him. It was then that we found out we had run into one of the famous celebrities of America's Great Loop, the man known by the locals as "The Conch King." He then proceeded to play complete musical songs on the conch shell which sounded like he was playing a trumpet. It was so enjoyable that none of the boats wanted the lock to open right away. He had Kathy attempt what he had done, but enough said about that. We thanked him for the entertainment and he received a big round of applause from all the boaters and we proceeded on our way with another wonderful boating memory.

FEAR KNOT

PHOTOS

Alligator River Marina

Enjoying fresh strawberries in the Florida sun

Belhaven, North Carolina courtesy car

The beautiful Dismal Swamp

The Dismal Swamp Conch King

ICW Cruise Ship hard aground

FEAR KNOT

Spotting Crab pots in the sun

Chesapeake Bay container barge & tow

Some slips take a little experience to get into

GENE SCHNAGL

CHAPTER 14 – THE BIG BAYS

Day 216 – After leaving the Dismal Swamp we were now back in salt water and a short distance up we turned into the Elizabeth River that took us into Norfolk, Virginia where we had a reservation at the waterside marina. We plan on spending a few days here to do some sightseeing which we are looking forward to. Besides, there are heavy northeast winds on the Chesapeake Bay and many boats are turning back to wait the weather out in Norfolk.

Not too far from our marina is a boat I looked at and thought, I would really like to buy that, but Kathy wouldn't let me. The boat is named the U.S.S. Wisconsin, the largest battleship ever built. What a beauty! I guess I'll just keep the boat I have for now, but I can dream, right? Besides, I'm not sure I could have got my trolling downriggers mounted on the stern.

Our location is great with everything to see and do in Norfolk. Also, for $1.00 (for us old people), we can take the ferry across the river to Portsmouth, Virginia and we have a whole other city to explore. Kathy is going crazy with all the shopping areas. Me, I'm just enjoying the sidewalk tables at all the coffee shops and the people watching.

We ran into some friends we made at the Alligator Marina in North Carolina so we will all be going to dinner together in Portsmouth, VA for our first night in town.

After enjoying Norfolk we started making our way toward Chesapeake Bay. The winds had died down and we were ready to be on the water again. Leaving the marina and rounding the point you suddenly see the largest naval base in the world. It is an awesome sight to behold. Huge naval vessels all along your starboard side and you are required to maintain your distance from them so we were sure to follow the boat traffic in the channel.

After passing the naval yards we entered Chesapeake Bay and made our turn to port for a planned 70 mile run to Deltaville, Virginia, our destination for this evening.

We arrived at Norview Marina and our timing was great as the weather turned very bad with tornado warnings in the surrounding area. Due to the poor weather we spent a couple of extra days here and unloaded the scooter again to explore the surrounding area.

During the storms two more boats arrived that we had met in Norfolk, so we went to dinner at a nearby restaurant that we were able to see up the shoreline from our slips. A limo from the restaurant picked us up and returned us making for a wonderful evening. Even though we could see the restaurant from the boats it was about a ten minute ride by land to get there over all the winding country roads.

The next morning we continued our voyage up the Chesapeake to the beautiful Solomon Islands where we had a reservation at the Hospitality Harbor Marina. The other boats from Deltaville joined us and we all planned on spending a couple of days here to enjoy the islands and relax.

After getting settled in the gals decided to do a little shopping and the guys spent their time cleaning the boats. I happened to notice that a lot of the crab boats were coming in so I went over to one of the boats and asked the Captain if he sold any crab right from the boat. He advised me that he not only sold the crab but he would sell me the boat if I wanted to buy it. I told him I didn't think I could get Kathy to work the pots so thanks anyway. I then bought 2 pounds of fresh caught lump crab meat and the Captain threw in a recipe for the best hot crab dip you have ever tasted. The gals hadn't planned on going out to dinner together until the next evening so I made a batch of the hot crab dip, opened a bottle of wine and got some specialty crackers out for Kathy and I before dinner. It was so good we ate that whole thing and that was our dinner that evening. I will be making this for years to come, I promise.

ANXIETY FACTOR – Are there any special cautions I should be aware of in the Chesapeake Bay area?

Actually there are a couple of things you want to be aware of while cruising these waters. First, with all the war ships in these waters, never approach a war ship within 100 yards without radio permission of the ship. Also maintain a no wake speed at all times within 500 yards of a war ship.

You may pass close to offshore facilities for unloading tanker ships such as Cove Point Offshore Fuel Terminal. There are Security Zones established around these facilities and they are well marked. Be sure that at no time you enter one of these zones.

Besides many container ships on the Chesapeake Bay, you will see many container barges being towed. Between the towboat and the huge container barge there are towing cables sometimes up to a quarter of a mile long. Do not maneuver your boat between a tow and a container barge at any time. Give domestic ships a lot of room and stay well clear.

Day 226 – We were going to head out of the Solomon's but the weather got a little bad again so we stayed an extra day. While walking along the docks we ran into another couple of old boating friends from back in Florida. They are from Toronto, Canada and wonderful people.

FEAR KNOT

Their boat is a trawler which they had anchored in the harbor area and had come ashore to provision in their dinghy. They found they had a leak in the dinghy so I helped him do the repair while the gals caught up on the news. They were leaving to go to another port so we agreed to try and meet up again in Annapolis, Maryland.

The next morning the weather cleared and we headed out to Annapolis, Maryland where we had reservations at the Horn Point Harbor Marina at East town in Annapolis. East town is a very historic area and a great place to stay for awhile.

I will be staying here for two weeks while Kathy flies home to Milwaukee, Wisconsin. She and our daughter are closing on the purchase of a new jewelry business and Deedee and I will be protecting the port of Annapolis.

While staying in Annapolis it gave me a lot of time to catch up on the boat. I changed the engine oil & filters, cleaned a lot of stainless and generally spent a time getting the boat looking good. I also used the scooter to sight see the city and head over to the Naval Academy. What a great area of history.

A few days before Kathy returned I had a little problem. I had secured the scooter at the end of the main dock for the night. In the morning I took Deedee out and the scooter was gone. It had been stolen during the night. I notified the Police and filed a report and thought that would be the end of it. They thought they were pretty sure where they might find it and advised they would let me know if they located it. What could I say; bad things happen now and then, no matter where you go.

ANXIETY FACTOR – Do we have to worry about crime very much on The Great Loop?

In the world we live in today sometimes bad things happen. There is no way to guarantee that a theft or vandalism problem won't occur. The best way to prevent any problems is being alert and knowing our surroundings whether we are staying in a slip or at anchor.

The theft we incurred was unusual for the community we were staying at in Annapolis. The Police did locate the scooter the very day we left and recovered it. Three minors were charged with the theft and handled within the court system. Things like this are going to happen no matter where you are and again, are rare on the waterways.

Keep your boat secure and check with the marine management regarding any issues in the area. If anchoring out check your waterway guides and talk to the locals when you pick up supplies or refuel, regarding any problems in the surrounding areas.

Boat theft is very rare and usually involves the theft of very high speed boats. The type of boat used by Loopers is not quite the type of boats thieves tend to want.

The application of common sense and alertness tends to make crime on the water not much of an issue.

Day 239 – Kathy had returned from her business trip, the boat was ready and we headed out again. It turned out to be a hot and humid day but the water was calm and we made our way to the Baltimore, Maryland Harbor. We had made reservations at the Baltimore City Docks and found it to be a great location to stay with easy access to the downtown Baltimore areas. Kathy did some shopping while Deedee and I rested our eyelids onboard. We then enjoyed a nice dinner at the Cheese Factory restaurant on the waterfront and called it a day.

Day 240 – Another nice morning and we headed out once again. I made a fuel stop at the Rusty Scupper Marina in Baltimore to top off and then moved on. As we left the harbor we again passed Fort McHenry where the battle with the British was fought that inspired the writing of the Star Spangled Banner. America's Great Loop is a constant visit into the history of this

great nation that just isn't seen in any other way except on the water.

North of Baltimore we crossed the Bay to the east shoreline as we would be entering the C&D Canal to cross over to the Delaware Bay. As we approached the canal I saw that we had a green light so we headed right on in. The C&D Canal is narrow and should a ship or tow with barges be in the canal others cannot pass. For this reason there are traffic lights at each end of the canal and at the marina entrances into the canal. If you get a red light you must wait for canal traffic to clear. It's just like driving on the streets, except no pot holes!

About half way down the canal we pulled into Summit Marina to spend the evening. The reason it is called Summit is that the Marina is at the bottom of a cliff. So to get up to the offices, etc. you have golf carts available and you just ride up the paths. It is a really interesting place to stay.

Day 241 – After making sure we had a green light again, we reentered the C&D and headed out into Delaware Bay. We found that the changing tides are pretty strong in the Bay and can have a big affect on the fuel consumption of your boat. With the tide, I gained two knots and against it, I lost three knots.

FEAR KNOT

Cruising was great until about 12 miles from Cape May, New Jersey. First I ran into a fog bank and there was a lot of heavy shipping around us. It didn't last very long and I was able to monitor traffic on radar so we had no problems. Then the weather changed abruptly and the winds picked up strong. Before too long we were running in about four foot seas off our Starboard quarter and eating a lot of spray. All in all it wasn't that bad and we made our way, right on course, into the channel at Cape May, New   Jersey.

GENE SCHNAGL

PHOTOS

Our slip at Cape May, New Jersey

ICW and Atlantic inlet double marker

FEAR KNOT

Nice boat but Kathy wouldn't let me buy it

Salt sprav takes its toll

Navy security is tight at Norfolk

It got a little rough off the New Jersey coast in the Atlantic

The calm Atlantic heading into the New York shipping channel

CHAPTER 15 – NEW JERSEY COASTLINE

Upon entering the Cape May channel we did run into a slight problem. There sat a large dredge directly in front of me blocking the channel. I contacted him by radio requesting a pass and he advised I should just pass through a narrow gap off his stern and we should be ok. We made the pass just fine and I was glad that he granted us the immediate pass so we didn't have to tread water in the high winds.

A short distance later we pulled into our slip at Miss Chris Marina in Cape May, New Jersey.

After getting tied up, Kathy explored Cape May with Deedee and I got all the salt spray washed off the boat again. Tomorrow we plan to head toward Atlantic City, New Jersey but the weather is saying thunderstorms, we'll have to wait and see.

We did have one incident during our stay in Cape May. Docked next to us was a Whale Watching boat for tourists. Now I'm not the smallest guy on the planet by any standard. Yet I did have a talk with the Captain of the Whale watching boat and advised him that if one more of his passengers pointed at me and yelled "Whale Ho" again that he and I were going to have a serious talk. Ok, just kidding, but it could have happened, right?

Day 242 – The thunderstorms were super heavy all night but we woke to just heavy overcast. We decided to make a go of it and see how far we could get, as we just couldn't seem to get a clear day.

With the high wind we decided that we would stay in the ICW rather than going off the coast. This made for some very slow going with the very shallow water and I was sucking a lot of mud into the sea strainers again. There was a lot of shoaling and the channel markers were not in the proper locations according to the charts and chart plotter. We were just going to have to feel our way along as the bad weather was supposed to last for days.

We also ran into a lot of crab pots in the channel areas. There were also many small fishing boats anchored directly in the channels which made passage extremely hazardous. Allowing for the obstructions we managed to continue on our way with a somewhat zigzag course.

At a number of the inlets I thought about trying to go out onto the Atlantic, but conditions were just too rough to take the chance. Besides that

FEAR KNOT

I found a number of the inlets blocked by shoaling and we had to turn back into the ICW. After struggling along for the day we decided to call it and pulled into the All Seasons Marina at Ocean City, New Jersey, where we were fortunate to get a slip for the night. It had been a very long day. There was an inlet just north of us, so the following morning I planned to check the weather data buoys offshore and try to make it out into the Atlantic.

Come the morning, the weather remained the same. We made one attempt to go out into the Atlantic, but had to turn back due to very rough sea conditions. We continued our travel up the New Jersey ICW toward Manasquan, New Jersey. It is here that the New Jersey ICW ends and you have no choice but to go out into the Atlantic to continue on to New York.

We had anticipated staying in Manasquan and waiting for a weather break, but as we traveled during the day, the weather started to break. By the time we arrived in Manasquan the winds had settled and the sun came out. I guess the Sea Gods were with us as we headed out offshore along the New Jersey coast.

We traveled about two miles off shore in about four foot rolling swells which made for a very comfortable ride. It was a ride through history for me as I had been stationed at Fort Monmouth, New Jersey for training when I had been in the Army and had spent a lot of time along the Jersey shores. It was great to be back again.

As we neared the New York coast line I turned into the New York shipping channel with a number of large cargo ships and tankers coming in from the ocean. We just kind of slid into the parade and followed them in. It wasn't going to be long and we would pass under the Verrazano Bridge at the Narrows and enter New York Harbor.

ANXIETY FACTOR – *I have heard a lot of stories of boaters having many problems trying to cruise the New Jersey ICW. Should I stay out of the ICW and stay off shore?*

I'm sorry to say that based on our experience I would recommend that you cruise off shore along this coast if weather and sea conditions permit. I found the ICW along New Jersey to be poorly maintained with improperly placed markers, etc.

Having said that, I would recommend that at the time you are planning on traveling this route you check your resources such as AGLCA, Coast Guard, Waterway Guides, etc. and obtain up to date condition information. Changes do happen and I'm sure some of the problems we incurred have been remedied.

Should you encounter similar conditions, do not worry, take it slow and easy inside or just plan on waiting out the weather and head off shore when conditions permit. Either way you will have a safe and enjoyable cruise up the New Jersey waters which offer many beautiful and scenic sights along the way.

GROUND ZERO IN THE SUN REFLECTION - NEVER FORGET!

GENE SCHNAGL

CHAPTER 16 – NEW YORK AND INLAND

This point in America's Great Loop has to be one of the most inspiring sights in your life. You experience a moment that has changed many of our ancestor's lives forever as they came to this country for the first time.

As Kathy and I crossed under the Verrazano Bridge we could see ahead of us the Statue of Liberty and Ellis Island directly ahead of us. To our right we could see Manhattan and the site of 9/11. We actually had tears in our eyes with the understanding of what we were looking at and what we had accomplished as a couple. Our journey wasn't over, but we had completed a large portion of a journey that only a very special group of individuals get to experience. We were members of the Association of America's Great Loopers and we were realizing a dream.

We maneuvered our way thru the heavy boat traffic in the harbor area and headed into the Hudson River. We then pulled into the Newport Yacht Club Marina at Jersey City, New Jersey. Then it dawned on me; it wouldn't be long and we would be in fresh water again until we returned home. It was going to be quite a change with no more tides and no more salt spray, but it would be a day or two until that happened.

ANXIETY FACTOR – We're from the Midwest and have heard that the boat traffic in New York harbor can be very dangerous. Is this something we should worry about?

New York harbor is like any other harbor you will experience in any large port. Yes, there is heavy boat traffic of all sizes, from transports down to kayaks. The one thing I would advise is that you will be tempted to sight see and not keep your eyes on the traffic surrounding you. Being alert is something you must concentrate on in this area. There are many car ferries and water taxis running back and forth in the harbor up until about 6:00pm. Keep your mind on what you are doing and your surroundings at all times. Also, watch for the wakes from some of these vessels and be prepared to turn into them so you are not surprised. The car ferries move along at a pretty good clip in the harbor area. Enjoy the city and welcome back to inland boating!

Day 246 – After settling in at the Newport Yacht Club we started our exploring and checked out Jersey City. The next morning we took the PATH train under the Hudson River from the terminal right next to our marina. We arrived at "Ground Zero" in Manhattan and spent the day enjoying our visit and saying a few prayers at the same time for those lost in the 9/11 event. As Kathy and I are both retired Law Enforcement it became a very emotional day as well. We went to Fire Station #10, directly across the street from where the Twin Towers

stood and had an opportunity to speak to one of the firemen and one of the police officers who survived that tragic day. We said a prayer together and wished each other well. I guess all I can say is, God Bless all who lost their lives that day and their families.

After a couple of great days in New York and New Jersey, including some fantastic deli food, we decided to push on again. We headed up the Hudson River toward our next destination of Haverstraw, New Jersey. We first decided to wait for a flow tide as the tides have a big pull on the Hudson River and we didn't want to burn up a bunch of fuel, fighting an ebb tide. It turned out to be a good decision and we were on our way with the incoming tide pushing us along.

The day was spent enjoying the beauty of the Hudson River even in the overcast and sometimes rainy weather. It was really nice to be back in the rivers again. In the late afternoon we arrived at the Haverstraw, New Jersey Marina and settled in for the night. The next morning it was raining so hard that we decided to stay one more day which turned out to be a good decision. It just didn't stop pouring all day and night.

The morning was still overcast but the rain was light so we headed out. We continued north and eventually arrived at Kingston, New York where we had reserved a slip. Kingston is a quaint, little, friendly town and we enjoyed our stay here. The marina, however, is designed for small boats and getting tied up took a little extra skill as the finger dock was only as long as half the length of our boat.

In the morning I did some calling around and we found out that due to all the rain they had closed access to the Erie Canal and boats were getting backed up, which meant marinas and anchoring areas were filling up. We called ahead and reserved a slip at the docks in Troy, New York and found out we had one of the few reservations remaining. We then set out to make it to Troy.

Going was slow up the Hudson in the continuing rain as the river was high and we were running against the strong currents. There was also a lot of boat and shipping traffic along the way. It was going to take some extra fuel but it would be worth it to be in position for the Erie Canal opening.

We made it to Troy, New York and got tied up in the strong currents on the river. The docks run parallel along the east bank of the Hudson just below the Federal Lock & Dam #1 which causes very strong currents along the dock. We put on a couple of extra dock lines just to be on the safe side with the high water conditions.

Directly above the Troy docks is a large city parking lot where we found they had their local Farmer's Market going on so we grabbed Deedee and headed off. Even in the rain it was a great time and we stocked up on some fresh produce and a couple of goodies.

I decided to check with the Erie Canal office regarding the Locks so I gave them a call. They were going to try and open things up, but it would depend on the rain again. We decided to stay one more night to see what happened.

The following day I checked with the Erie Canal office and again they advised they would be open tomorrow. They also advised me that there was a tow with barges that was going to try and head up the Erie to get to Canada and I might want to get in ahead of him if I could, as I wouldn't be able to pass him for a long way on the canal. With this advice we decided we would head out early in the morning and get into the lock ahead of the tow. We just hoped the rain would work with us on this.

GENE SCHNAGL

PHOTOS

Liberty dead ahead

Ellis Island

Manhattan from the Newport Yacht Club, Jersey City, New Jersey

FEAR KNOT

God Bless America

Fast moving Hudson River traffic

Short slip at Kingston, New York Marina

CHAPTER 17 – THE ERIE AND OSWEGO CANALS

Morning arrived with no rain but plenty of wind. The currents on the Hudson were still extremely strong so we let go our lines and got ourselves out into the river. We headed into Federal Lock #1 which would put us in position to go to Lake Champlain or turn left into the Erie Canal, which was where we were headed. We passed the tow and barges tied up on the lock entry wall and treaded water for a few minutes until the lock opened. This was going to be our first of ten locks this day, if we were lucky.

The first eight locks on the Erie are so close together that you just seem to go out of one and into the next. For this reason you just leave your locking fenders and lines in place as you move from one to the next. Normally leaving your fenders out while cruising makes you look like a novice, but in this case it is necessary.

The Erie Canal is a beautiful waterway that is a pleasure to cruise on and we were enjoying the surrounding beauty as we made our way through the locks. Then, naturally, a little problem came up again.

As we got nearer to Lock #8 the winds started to pick up rapidly. We were getting gusts between 30-40 mph. In Lock #8 we were told to tie starboard which we and the large motor yacht in front of us both did. The locking process here is to grab a wall lock line fore and aft and just hang on. You are also required to shut your engines down while locking. In the high wind gusts Kathy could not hold the line and it was yanked from her hand resulting in us being pulled off the lock wall. I was able to run to the bridge, start the engines, and correct the boat as the boat in front of us with three men on board pulled off as well.

In Lock #9 this occurred again to both boats and in Lock #10 we advised the Lockmaster that we didn't want to tie starboard and would go port which he finally agreed to. Our reason for this was that on Lock #9 Kathy had taken a wrap on a cleat with the line because of the high winds and the line had torn off the lock wall. I guess we had enough locking for one day.

ANXIETY FACTOR – *Is locking difficult in the New York Canals?*

Locking in the New York Canals is not any different than any other locks. In fact, you will find it much easier than the Mississippi, Ohio, and Tennessee Locks as you don't have the heavy commercial boat traffic on the New York Canals.

In our case we had extreme wind conditions and should probably have tied up and waited out the weather. The incidents we experienced were a result of our decisions so I would recommend that should you experience these conditions make your decisions based on what you know at that time and what works best for you.

After clearing Lock #10 we decided to stop in Amsterdam, New York for the night and tied up on the city dock wall. We met with some fellow boaters and sat on the dock with "refreshments" and shared experiences. A nice quiet evening and a good night's sleep followed; tomorrow's another day.

We awoke to sunshine and mild breezes, things were finally looking up. I knew we were really going to enjoy this day. With the milder weather the canal traffic picked up, but it was easy going and transiting the locks went as easy as could be. Now we could really enjoy the beauty of the Erie Canal. We continued locking until we reached Little Falls, New York where we had reserved a slip at the New York State Marina.

With the good weather it gave me a chance to check out the damage to the boat from the lock experiences. It seems it is just a little gel coat work which can be attended to when we return home. I did get a chance to check on the motor yacht with us and they took some heavier damage to their port side rails as well as their hull. I guess that's what boating is all about. Everyone gets a nick now and then, so not to worry!

ANXIETY FACTOR – *I've heard that entering locks around dams in high water is dangerous, is this correct?*

Whenever you enter a lock you need to use caution. However, during high water conditions you will find the water is usually pouring heavily over the dam or from the sluice gates beside the lock. If you experience this condition be especially alert.

Keep your eyes on the water and watch for eddies forming and the flow of the current. If it is flowing across your bow be prepared to over steer and correct as you enter the lock. These currents can sometimes spin your boat if you are not prepared for them. Just be ready and, with experience, you will learn to read the water and will anticipate the changes, leaving you with minimal problems on your lock entry.

We did have one incident where a trawler was in front of us entering a lock, when the side current spun his vessel out of control. The Captain regained control but had to go back behind us and reenter. As we entered I corrected for the side current and we went right into the lock. Be a Boy Scout and be prepared!

Day 254 – Today was a really enjoyable, uneventful day. The weather was great and boat traffic was moving just fine. Also, there are really no bugs; we must be headed north again! Later in the day we arrived at Sylvan

FEAR KNOT

Beach Marina, New York on the south shores of Lake Oneida.

It has been an interesting few days on the Erie Canal. We have transited 22 locks on the canal and now arrived at a shallow lake, Lake Oneida, which is 20 miles long. After crossing the lake tomorrow we will reach the last lock on the Erie Canal and then turn north again on the Oswego Canal where we will have 7 more locks until we finally reach Lake Ontario.

Day 255 – We crossed Lake Oneida on a perfect day; the water was as flat as glass. The mid lake shoals were well marked and we reached Brewerton, New York Lock #23 without incident. We made our way through the lock and then continued for a few miles turning north on the Oswego Canal.

ANXIETY FACTOR – Are there any special cautions for the Oswego Canal Locks?

The Oswego Canal locks pose no problems for most boats except for large motor yachts that have a lot of distance between the main deck and the waterline.

The locks utilize a rope tie for your boat that is secured to the lock wall. If the lock is full when you enter, which they always are when headed north as the Oswego Canal goes down to Lake Ontario, then the rope will be just above the waterline where you have to reach for it. This is very difficult for large motor yachts where your deck is high above the lock wall.

To avoid any issues be sure to have a dock pole available for the line tenders on your boat and they will be able to reach the rope and pull it to them without a problem.

After completing the remaining Oswego locks we arrived at the Oswego Marina and tied up at our slip. The next step was to prepare to leave America and head into Canada.

FEAR KNOT

PHOTOS

Beautiful Erie Canal

Kathy's Erie Canal storm souvenir

GENE SCHNAGL

I think this is a new Iranian gunboat

Tied up at Troy, New York

Approaching an Oswego Canal Lock

**Kathy feeling a little sunstroke on the Erie Canal
after a hard day on deck locking**

Locking on the Oswego Canal

GENE SCHNAGL

CHAPTER 18 – CANADA

When departing Oswego, New York we had two options to enter Canada. We could either follow the New York coast east on Lake Ontario to the Thousand Islands area. This is a beautiful area to spend time in and is the route I would highly recommend. If we did this we would be clearing Canadian customs at Kingston, Ontario, Canada. The second option was to cross the center of Lake Ontario and take the Murray Canal to cut through to the Bay of Quinte and then clear customs at Trenton, Ontario, the starting point of the Trent-Severn Waterway. We decided to cross the lake and head directly to Trenton.

ANXIETY FACTOR – How do we prepare to leave the country and enter into Canada?

In today's world you will need to be sure that you meet all the new security requirements for leaving the United States and returning.. This also applies to entering and leaving Canada. Rules are changing all the time in both nations and can get a little confusing.

My best recommendation is complete your research carefully. The best way I have found to do this is by joining the America's Great Loop Cruisers' Association. They can provide you with up to date information of exactly what will be required and show you how to comply without any issues. I would also suggest that you attend one of the AGLCA Rendezvous' prior to your Loop departure. You will find many resources available to you as well as many experienced Loop boaters to provide you with answers to your questions. Be sure you have a current passport for every person on board as this is an absolute requirement now.

Day 256 – We are finally ready to cross Lake Ontario. The wind is up a little, giving us about 3-4 foot seas but the cruising should be fine, even with the spray. We will be taking on the wind screen. As we worked our way across Lake Ontario we found it interesting that it wasn't until mid-lake that we spotted our first vessel on the water, a large transport ship. It turned out that it was the only vessel we saw during the entire crossing of the lake.

We crossed without incident and entered the first lock on the Murray Canal. This is a canal about five miles in length that takes you into the Bay of Quinte and Trenton, Ontario, Canada. As the lock opened to let us into the canal the operator came out to the lock wall with a long pole with a cup on the end of it which he proceeded to hold out to Kathy who was on the front deck. We had previously been made aware that there is a $5.00 U.S. fee to transit the lock and had been prepared. Kathy placed the $5.00 in the cup and we were on our way to the next lock. Had she not placed the money in the cup the operator would not have been too excited.

He would have just made a call and the Canadian Police would have been waiting at the closed lock ahead for us, collected the money and given us a gift of a citation to go along with the fee. It seemed like a pretty good system and it works very well.

We made it through the second lock with no waiting and entered the Bay of Quinte. A little twisting and turning around some rocky shoals and weed beds and we pulled into Trenton, Ontario Marina. We were starting another leg of our adventure and were really looking forward to it.

We had called ahead by radio and the Harbormaster had given us directions to a slip. After we were tied up Kathy and Deedee stayed onboard as required by law, and I, as Captain, went to the Marina office with all our papers and made a phone call to Canadian Customs as required. After answering a number of questions I was given, our Customs clearance number and returned to our boat so Kathy could come ashore with Deedee for Deedee's long anticipated stroll in the park.

Day 259 – Trenton, Ontario is a great port with everything you need within walking distance. The waterfront area is totally designed with transient boaters in mind. We walked into town and I got a haircut while Kathy got her nails done again. We then did some shopping to restock the boat, had some lunch downtown and then headed back.

In the early evening a small crowd of local people came to the park just next to our slip and started setting up lawn chairs around a small gazebo. When we inquired what the event was, we found out that they had music in the park in the evenings. So we fixed ourselves a drink and sat on the aft deck and enjoyed the great music. It was a relaxing evening and we decided that we would stay an extra day to further explore the town and the people.

The next day some of the boating friends we had not seen since Norfolk, Virginia arrived at the marina. We all decided to go out to dinner and celebrate one of the wife's birthdays and had a great time. We were all excited about heading out on the famous Trent-Severn Waterway. Tomorrow would be a big day.

Well it's Sunday morning and we had some heavy rain last night but today looks just great. The only downside is that the temperatures are in the 90's and the humidity feels just as high. Also, the winds have picked up but we'll be just fine in these smaller locks.

FEAR KNOT

We have thirteen locks to make in the first 31 miles; it should be an interesting day. The Trent-Severn locks are beautiful and actually fun to lock through. The boat traffic is a little heavy, but the locking system runs very efficiently and we experienced no problems.

In the early afternoon Kathy started feeling a little sick. I think it may be some heatstroke in all this high temperature and humidity so I will call it a short day today. I pulled into the City docks at Campbellsford, Ontario and we got tied up. The winds were strong but we made it in without too much trouble.

I hooked up the shore power to turn on the air conditioning and get Kathy cooled down, but the shore circuit breakers keep shutting off due to the high power demands in the area from all the heat. I then started the generator and let Kathy and the dog cool down and get some rest which made us all feel better. I set about getting the boat cleaned up and spent time talking with some of the other boaters pulling in for the night. It was a time to relax and stay out of the heat.

ANXIETY FACTOR – When docking on a river with strong current but high wind blowing the opposite direction which direction should I dock from?

This situation can cause you some concern but it can be worked out just fine if you take a good look at what is going on. As we pulled into Campbellsford, Ontario we were headed into the current on the river. With all the recent rain the water was very high and the current very strong. Normally I would have approached the dock wall into the current for a portside tie up. The problem we had is that we also had very high winds but from the opposite direction. This is where knowing your boat comes into play.

With a high enclosed bridge like our boat wind has a huge affect on the handling of the vessel, unlike a sailboat or a low cruisers style. For this reason I chose to go past my docking area and turn into the wind to approach the landing. Based on previous experience with our boat I felt this was the safest approach. Even with the strong current, it allowed me better control of the boat and we came in without a problem.

Getting to know your boat is very important and with a little experience you will be able to judge your responses for situations like this.

Day 259 – It was lucky that we decided to call it a day early yesterday. Not only did it help Kathy feel better, but it rained all night and into this morning. We are on our way again and will see just how far we get in this damp weather. Visibility is still ok so we will continue on.

The first lock we hit was lock 13 and we ran into a minor problem. We couldn't find anyone operating the lock. We waited while the boats started to pile up behind us so Kathy went ashore and walked up to the lock offices but

still couldn't find anyone around. After about 45 minutes a truck pulled into the office area and we were informed that the operator at lock 14 had gotten ill. For that reason the operator at lock 13 was running both locks this morning until they could find a replacement for Lock 14.

What he was required to do now was to open lock 13 and allow as many boats as possible in. In our case he wanted four boats in but we convinced him that only three would fit without damage as one was a sailboat and we kind of towered over him. He then filled the lock, let us out, closed the lock behind us again and then he drove up to lock 14 to meet us.

At that point he opened lock 14, got us all in, then filled the lock and let us out again. He then proceeded to drive back to lock 13 and start the process over. It took about three hours to get the three boats through the two locks and we really felt sorry for the operator, but at least we were on our way again with nothing lost but a little time.

ANXIETY FACTOR – IS IT DIFFICULT TO TRANSIT THE TRENT-SEVERN WATERWAYS?

The Trent-Severn Waterway is some of the most beautiful and scenic water you will cruise on in your lifetime. The waterway was constructed utilizing unique locking systems, natural lakes, rivers, and manmade canals. As such, caution is needed in some of the areas as much of this design was done in the 19th century and was done with much smaller vessels in mind. Many of the channels are so narrow that two boats cannot pass side to side and one will have to give way.

All that being said just means you will have to pay a little more attention to your surroundings as you move along. You also do not want to go aground on the granite bottom as it is very unforgiving unlike the coastal sand and mud. The water is normally very clear so you can see the granite ledges along the shoreline. Just keep your vessel centered and under control and enjoy the natural beauty of your surroundings.

We continued on our way but as we did so the winds started kicking up again and in the narrow channels I had some difficulty keeping the boat centered and away from the rocky shorelines. After Lock 18 we decided to call it a day early and tied up at Hastings, Ontario.

In hind sight this was a very good decision as the skies got very dark and opened up on us. We got hit with torrential rains and large hail. It didn't last that long but everything above deck was a wet mess and blown around. We did some cleaning up and hit the bunks early. Tomorrow was sure to be a better weather day as it couldn't be any worse.

Day 262 – Over the next few days we continued to see nothing but eye stunning scenery. I must admit it felt a little awkward piloting a multi-ton vessel through waters that I used to canoe on.

FEAR KNOT

It gives a Captain a wonderful feeling of accomplishment as you maneuver your way along these glacial trails.

We finally arrived in Bobcaygeon, Ontario, a beautiful little town along the river, and tied up at the Gordon Yacht Harbor. They had Wi-Fi available so I was able to catch up on some blog entries after days being out of internet contact. There are many days up here where you have to remember that you are truly in God's country and He just doesn't need the internet much.

At this point we are about two days out of Georgian Bay and will reach the end of all the locks for our America's Great Loop. It is becoming hard to believe that we have traveled this   far.

GENE SCHNAGL

PHOTOS

The only traffic on Lake Ontario crossing, one freighter

The Murray Canal five dollar lock cup

Trenton, Ontario customs & downtown

FEAR KNOT

Narrow channels on the Trent-Severn

Be alert for approaching traffic

Some lock gates are a little snug

Petersboro lift lock

Trent-Severn step lock

Don't get out of the channel

Big Chute railroad lock

Headed over Big Chute

GENE SCHNAGL

I hope nobody flushes while we are in there

Kathy searching for missing lock attendant

Going down Kirkfield lift lock

FEAR KNOT

Watch carefully for Trent-Severn channel markers

Only 18 inches under the keel at Snug Harbor

Snuggled up safe at Snug Harbor

GENE SCHNAGL

CHAPTER 19 – GEORGIAN BAY/NORTH CHANNEL

After a few more locks we arrived at the last lock in Severn, Ontario. We had completed the Trent-Severn Waterway and were headed back into the Great Lakes. It was going to be nice to be back in the deep water again.

You may have noticed that I did not write about the unique locks along the Trent-Severn such as the Peterborough Lift Lock, the Kirkfield Lift Lock or the Big Chute Rail Lock. The reason I didn't is that it would take another book just to begin to describe how exciting it is to transit this area. Just one trip through and you have lasting memories you just can't stop talking about. In your Great Loop preparation you will find a lot to read about regarding this area and in doing so you will find yourself well prepared to handle them with ease, as well as great anticipation.

We cleared the last lock and then turned north along the east shoreline of Georgian Bay. We had decided that rather than cross the south end of the Bay or follow the southern shoreline to the opposite coast, that we would travel through the Thirty Thousand Island area of the east coast and cross the bay on the north end.

ANXIETY FACTOR – *I've heard it can be dangerous traveling up the east coast of Georgian Bay, should I be concerned?*

The east coast of Georgian Bay is known as the Thirty Thousand Islands for a good reason. There are thousands of rock shoals both above and just below the surface of the water. Should you strike one of these you will, without a doubt, damage your boat.

Having said that, the coastal channel is well marked as it weaves its way throughout the islands. Your charts and Waterway Guides will keep you on track and advise you of the best harbors and anchorages along the way.

Keep alert as usual and watch your route and you will have a scenic and safe transit all the way up the coast.

We traveled up the east coast of Georgian Bay following the channel markers through the shoals. This is an exciting and beautiful area with lots of wildlife to be seen as you go. For a northern boy, like myself, I was home again and I was at peace.

We had made a reservation at a marina tucked back into a bay off the coast called Snug Harbor. Having never been there before we didn't know what to expect so we would just have to see what was waiting for us.

I turned into a small bay and finally came around a point into a narrow channel. It was then we discovered that the marina was at a small village that had never seen a vessel the size of ours come into their harbor. The only dock they had, where we would partly fit, was their fuel dock and the channel in to it only allowed 18 inches of water under our keel. The town people at the marina/restaurant all came out to watch us come in so I decided I wouldn't disappoint them by departing, so it was slow speed ahead. I was able to get the boat in and turned and up to the dock with about 25 people trying to assist on shore and all taking pictures at the same time. The marina owners and town people were super friendly and we had dinner at the restaurant with all the locals, although it is a little difficult eating dinner, getting your picture taken and answering questions at the same time. Deedee had plenty of local dogs to play with, but Kathy had to walk to the top of a small mountain to make a cell phone call as the village is so secluded they couldn't get TV or cell reception down at lake level. It was still a wonderful and memorable stop and we did not regret our decision to stay.

The next day we continued north and had perfectly flat water on the Bay which is very unusual. With this opportunity I decided to find a gap through the islands to cross the Bay. I soon discovered that this is harder than it looks, as even though I saw a gap I soon found that there was another shoal just under the surface of the water wherever I tried to slip through. I continued following the markers until we reached an inlet entering into the Bay and we then turned and crossed.

After a 60 mile crossing of the Bay we arrived at the entrance to the North Channel at Killarney, Ontario. We followed the channel in and tied up at the Sportsman's Club dock. We had made a reservation here and it was lucky we had as there was a lot of boat traffic in the area and the marina was filling up fast.

We were soon joined by the boat from Michigan that we had traveled with along the Erie Canal with the three guys aboard. In the afternoon we found out one of them had fallen onboard and been injured and needed to go to a hospital. The Marina called for an ambulance and we agreed that Kathy would go with him to the hospital. The hospital is so far away that they didn't get back to the marina until around two in the morning. In the end it turned out that he wasn't injured that bad, but it was worth the time and trip to be on the safe side.

ANXIETY FACTOR – If we should have a medical issue while in Canada will our medical insurance cover us?

Canada's medical program does not accept American medical insurance. If you should require medical treatment they have set fees for services and will accept a credit card. You will then have to contact your insurance provider in the states to seek reimbursement from them.

It is best to contact your medical provider before starting your journey into Canada and discuss the best procedures for you. Medical services in Canada are good and you will not have to worry about any treatment you receive.

Day 266 – We departed Killarney and continued west along the North Channel. We had one more obstacle to get by before we had clear cruising all the way to our slip in Milwaukee, Wisconsin. That was the lift bridge at Little Current, Ontario. The bridge opens on the hour so we needed to time it right.

As we approached the lift bridge I could see that it was open so I continued on. As I got near it I saw it start to close so I contacted the operator and requested he hold for me. I was advised that he opened and closed on the hour and if you didn't make it you waited. He then closed the bridge and we "treaded" water for an hour until the next opening. I might point out at this point that during that hour not one vehicle passed over that bridge, but "rules is rules", right? This is true especially when you have the key to the bridge.

When the bridge finally opened I passed under quickly, just in case, and we proceeded on to Gore Bay Marina, Ontario where we had reserved a slip for the evening.

Gore Bay is a quaint little village located on Mantoulin Island, Ontario Canada. While I cleaned the boat, Kathy walked into town and met with some of the local people whom she found very friendly. Of course she did a little shopping while she was there.

In the morning, after fueling up, we decided to make a long run of about 80 miles and head back into the United States again. At this point we had a choice of either following the direct south edge of The North Channel or going along the much more picturesque north edge where all the small islands and fishing villages are located. As we had a time commitment we opted for the southern route, but I would surely recommend the northern route if you can.

We arrived at Drummond Island Customs and I went ashore to clear. All our papers were in order so Kathy quickly brought Deedee ashore. After we climbed back aboard we headed to the town of Detour, Ontario Marina.

ANXIETY FACTOR – _Will we have any problems clearing United States Customs when returning?_

As we discussed earlier in this book, when you prepare to leave the United States you will also be preparing to return to the United States at the same time. If you complete the proper procedures at that time the reentry will not be an issue.

You will be able to clear customs at either the north or south end of Drummond Island or now you can just proceed directly to Mackinac Island and clear by videophone at the marina fuel dock which you may find to be the easiest.

For Canadians entering the United States, be sure to check with U.S. Customs for entry requirements before entering and make sure to have everything completed to reenter Canada at a later date.

In Detour, Kathy walked into town to get a few groceries. She later returned with a full grocery cart. It seems she met a wonderful market owner in town. At Sune's Market in Detour she gave Kathy great boater discounts and told her she always welcomes boaters who stop in when traveling through. We surely won't forget to stop by when we return. After loading Kathy's "treasures" on the boat we settled in for the evening.

The following morning we cleared our lines and headed out to Mackinac Island. We were back in, what we considered, home waters again

GENE SCHNAGL

PHOTOS

Georgian Bay a sheet of glass

Watch for seaplanes landing over you in the North Channel

GENE SCHNAGL

CHAPTER 20 – LAKE MICHIGAN

We arrived at Mackinac Marina and got settled in. We then went ashore and enjoyed the beautiful and historic Mackinac village shops. After some shopping and a bite to eat we returned to the boat to relax and chart out the next day which would be on Lake Michigan. It was very exciting to know that in just days we were going to be home again after almost a year on the water. WOW! While I was sitting on the aft deck Deedee barked at something in the water and when I looked down there was a young otter playing in the clear water just aft of our swim platform. He would dive down, bring up a clam and a small rock and lay on his back to open it. I had a great time watching and Deedee had a great time trying to figure out what it was.

In the morning we pulled out and very quickly passed under the majestic Mackinac Bridge. The seas were up a little, running about three feet, but I guess that's what we call "flat" water on Lake Michigan. We made our turn south and headed out toward the very popular, Charlevoix, Michigan Marina.

As we came into the harbor channel at Charlevoix, I had to laugh because Kathy asked, "What's that?" up there. She thought she was all done going through locks and here was one more. Yes, there is a lock to enter into Charlevoix's inner harbor. We had to wait a little for the lock and finally made it in. The Harbormaster gave us a great tie up and we got settled down. After a shower and some clean clothes we headed into Charlevoix where Kathy was in seventh heaven with all the shops. This is a true "Lady Boaters" port. Deedee and I sat on the street benches and people watched while Kathy explored the many shops. What a great little town to stop at. I don't mind sitting on the benches waiting while Kathy shops if I have Deedee with me. I don't call her my "Chick Magnet" for nothing. The same principle works with grandchildren, but the dog is quieter.

After Kathy was shopped out we took Deedee back to the boat and headed out for dinner. Then it was a good night's sleep for everyone.

When we headed out the next morning our destination was Frankfort, Michigan, which was south of us and would be our crossing point for Lake Michigan. We decided to cross here as this is the narrowest crossing on Lake Michigan; from Frankfort, Michigan to Manitowoc, Wisconsin. As usual we ran into a weather issue. The wind started to pick up and the seas got up to about 4-5 feet so we decided to call it an early day and pull into the marina at Leland, Michigan about midway between Charlevoix and Frankfort.

Leland is a comfortable little marina that extends out into the main lake from the coast of Lake Michigan. With a seawall built around the harbor it is protected and was a good spot to stop and wait out the heavy seas. After getting securely tied up against the winds Kathy headed out shopping and Deedee and I relaxed ashore at the marina. I grabbed a cup of coffee and joined the other Captains for a shore side chat which always makes for a good time in a marina.

In the morning the waters had calmed so we headed to Frankfort, one of our favorite harbors on Lake Michigan. As with most of the Lake Michigan ports, Frankfort is another quaint small town that is very comfortable with lots of neat shops and restaurants. As it was such a short run from Leland we had lots of time to relax and enjoy the port. If the weather held out we would only have one more stop until we were in our own slip again.

The following morning the seas weren't that bad with maybe 2-3 foot waves. The advantage was that the wind was out of the northeast which would give us more of a following sea.

With home in mind we started our 79 mile crossing. All was going well until about mid-lake when the wind increased a little and the seas went up to around 4 feet. At that point I just changed our course to more southwest so we took it all off the stern and we were pushed nicely right into Manitowoc, Wisconsin Harbor. We had made it; we were back in our own state again.

It wasn't until we were tying up that we realized it was the 4th of July. I guess you kind of lose track of time and days on the water for so long. I washed down the boat and Kathy and I took showers. After which I made us some hors d'oeuvres and a drink and we settled down on the aft deck to enjoy the beautiful evening of fireworks. Deedee settled in on the deck with a new chew toy and life was wonderful. As we relaxed we started to reflect on what we had accomplished together and somehow it just didn't seem possible. I guess up until now we had just thought of the voyage as small pieces but now we could start to see the total picture and it was a little overwhelming. This would be the first of many evenings of quiet thought like this.

Later I prepared dinner for us on board and as the sun set we got out the deck chairs to sit on the docks and watch the fireworks with the other boaters in the marina. I guess this was going to be one of the most memorable Independence Days we would have in our lives and what made it even that much more special is what we had accomplished together.

The next morning we had calm seas and we set out on the final leg. We cruised south along the Wisconsin coast and pulled into Port Washington, Wisconsin, one of our local stops, to have lunch and refuel. After lunch we continued south and suddenly could see in the distance the tall buildings of Milwaukee, our home port.

To say we were getting excited is a true understatement. We didn't even talk to each other, but kept watching the buildings get closer and closer with each of us deep in our own thoughts.

It wasn't long and I rounded the north point and could see the Milwaukee Harbor before us. We were about three miles offshore at the time and I changed course and lined up with the north gap into the main harbor. I called McKinley Marina on the radio and advised that we were inbound and would be docking in about 15 minutes. The harbormaster welcomed us home and gave us a temporary slip close in to the seawall so we would have less trouble unloading some of our gear.

As we turned into the inner harbor Kathy went forward to get our lines out and fenders down. I looked down at her from the bridge and I could see her just standing on the forward deck staring at F dock, the dock we had last pulled out of almost a year ago. I couldn't help but wonder what she was thinking after all this time. I guess we were going to have numerous conversations over those thoughts in the days to come.

As I spun the boat and backed into our slip I couldn't help but wonder about how it seemed such an effortless procedure now that we had completed this long journey. My memory seemed to tell me that it was always somewhat more difficult just a year ago. I wonder why?

I maneuvered the boat into the slip and Kathy stepped off the swim platform onto the finger dock and secured the aft line. She then went forward and secured the bow line and I shut down the engine for the last time on this trip. "WE" had done it; we had completed AMERICA'S GREAT LOOP.

GENE SCHNAGL

EPILOGUE

After living on your boat for almost a year you find that life goes on and you pretty much return to normal, if there is such a state, very quickly. Yes, you are happy to be home and yes, everyone is happy to see each other. I guess that is to be expected. In our case it was pretty much the same.

Kathy has gone on and built her jewelry store business. She built it to the point that she has hired a number of new employees and just recently announced the opening of her new store specializing in an entirely different product line. She is very happy being a professional business woman again.

Deedee has returned to chasing squirrels and keeping our yard safe. She still wanders down into the creek behind our home but I think that is more out of curiosity than missing being on the water.

The Captain, well I'm enjoying life also. I have been putting on a number of seminars around Lake Michigan to boating organizations and yacht clubs encouraging others to think about doing America's Great Loop. Kathy and I also attend as many of the AGLCA Rendezvous' that we can, where I put on presentations regarding the different sections of the Loop. Hopefully I can assist the new members in completing their dream, as we did, and doing it with much less fear and anxiety than what we experienced.

As you can see I've also been doing a little writing over time. It's nice to keep "old people" busy.

Del Coronado, well she is still with us. She was birthed at the Milwaukee South Shore Yacht Club for a period of time but is now back in her old slip at Milwaukee's McKinley Marina at the main harbor. She has been tuned up, cleaned up and has all new canvas but she proudly flies the Gold AGLCA Burgee forward to tell all that she completed America's Great Loop.

Was it worth all the expense and time for what we did? Kathy and I have talked about this numerous times since our adventure and have decided that, in all honesty, yes it was! I think the most important gain was that we have found that bond between us tighten immensely as a result of the voyage. We learned that we were a team again and can function as one. I personally believe that over time in a marriage we are together but our accomplishments seem to be as individuals. America's Great Loop did not allow us to do that. You find that you must think and act as one to be successful and for that reason you get to share the pride and honor as one not as individuals. It is one of the accomplishments in our lives where we can say that, "we did it!"

It is important that you remember, all I've stated in this writing are suggestions based on our experience. Each of you must make yourselves aware of the rules, laws and requirements for safety that are available to you before departing. The more you educate yourselves and provide for your personal well being the safer and more enjoyable your voyage will be.

Will we do America's Great Loop again? Yes, if we can, we will. But as with everything in life, we have to see where life takes us. Until then we will continue to share our adventure and do our best to help others do the same.

We now owe so much to so many people who helped us along the way. So many people we will never forget in all the towns and harbors in two great nations. Yet, most of all we want to thank our fellow boaters who gave us so many hours of friendship and happy memories and especially America's Great Loop Cruisers' Association. Without this organization we

GENE SCHNAGL

would never have known what was waiting out there for us to enrich our lives forever. God bless you all and thank you from the bottom of our hearts.

God Bless America and Canada!

Smooth Seas!

FEAR KNOT

MILWAUKEE AND HOME ARE DEAD AHEAD!

GENE SCHNAGL

Made in the USA
Lexington, KY
17 September 2014